Books by Bob Chieger

INSIDE GOLF:
Quotations on the Royal and Ancient Game   1985

WAS IT GOOD FOR YOU, TOO?
Quotations on Love and Sex   1983

VOICES OF BASEBALL:
Quotations on the Summer Game   1983

Books by Pat Sullivan

INSIDE GOLF:
Quotations on the Royal and Ancient Game   1985

Inside Golf

Inside Golf:

Quotations on the Royal and
Ancient Game

Bob Chieger and
Pat Sullivan

Atheneum New York

Atheneum
Macmillan Publishing Company
866 Third Avenue, New York, NY 10022

Library of Congress Cataloging-in-Publication Data

Chieger, Bob.
  Inside golf.

  Bibliography: p.
  Includes index.
  1. Golf—Quotations, maxims, etc.   I. Sullivan,
Pat. II. Title.
GV965.C474   1985   796.352   84-45615
ISBN 0-689-11546-6

Macmillan books are available at special discounts for bulk purchases for sales promotions, premiums, fund-raising, or educational use. For details, contact:

        Special Sales Director
        Macmillan Publishing Company
        866 Third Avenue
        New York, NY 10022

13   12   11   10   9   8   7   6   5

Printed in the United States of America

Golfers talk a lot, and they talk very well as a rule. Out in the privacy of the course, invigorated by the sweet air and the spring of the turf, a man opens up. He speaks his mind candidly on almost any subject. Things strike him humorously, including himself.

Herbert Warren Wind
"The Lure of Golf," 1954

Contents

Introduction

The year was about 1100 A.D. The setting was a knoll in Scotland, perhaps next to one of the King's archery ranges. A sewn spheroid packed with feathers—the first golf ball—was whacked for the first time in history. Moments later, someone probably made a comment, perhaps what teaching professional Bob Toski calls the saddest words in golf:

"You're still away."

It is the nature of golf that a lot more words—of wit, of truth, and of mirth—are spoken than rounds played. This book contains a collection of utterances on golf—famous and newly discovered—gems of insight, random thoughts, and pointed statements that in sum, we trust, will inspire the reader to a finer appreciation of the game. And if we have achieved our purpose, perhaps the reader will find some advice contained within these nuggets to shave a stroke or two off his own game. Then we can all retire to the clubhouse.

Not long after it was invented, it became evident that golf had a peculiar hold on those who played it. Worried that the game was distracting the populace from its compulsory archery practice, the Scottish Parliament of King James II in 1457 issued a proclamation: "Golfe be utterly cryed down and not be used." Rather like government's attitude toward sex.

By 1600, Parliament had backed down somewhat, forbidding golf only during the Sunday hours of "devine services." By the middle of the eighteenth century, golf's reputation among the educated classes hadn't improved much. "It is unjust to claim the privileges of age," remarked Dr. Samuel Johnson on the game, "and retain the playthings of childhood." Finally, in the twentieth century, Canadian economist and humorist Stephen Butler Leacock put the game in its proper perspective. "Golf may be played on Sunday," he wrote, "not being a game within the view of the law, but being a form of moral effort."

Today some of our finest golf is played on Sundays, the traditional day of the final round every week on the magnificent professional golf tours. But it was on a Friday during the second round of the Western Open that Lee Trevino was struck and seriously injured by lightning. When asked if golf clubs didn't serve as lightning rods, he struck back with his own wit. "Even God," said Trevino, "couldn't hit a one-iron."

When it comes to mishitting the ball, one would think the memorable comments would come from hackers; but that's not the case. George Bayer, a powerful driver who would hit the ball so far—and so wildly—that he once asked Arnold Palmer how to *reduce* his length, would understand Jim Dent's comment, "I can airmail the ball, but sometimes I don't put the right address on it." Or consider Miller Barber's dilemma in trying to find the proper fairway: "I don't say my game is bad," he said, "but if I grew tomatoes they'd come up sliced."

Beauty, grace, balance, harnessed energy, self-control, and deep concentration are all elements of the golf swing. The problem—and golf's paradox—is that such perfection can never be sustained. Out of that conflict flows the words. Baseball, a game of similar eloquence, allows a career for a man who hits the ball well—a base hit—just one out of four times, the .250 hitter. In this respect baseball resembles golf, where a man can shoot seventy and still have delivered only a dozen well-stroked balls in the round.

But for some of us, even a mediocre round can be saved by playing with the right people, for the well-turned phrase can give us as much pleasure as the well-hit ball. And golf seems to provide the phrases, for as writer John Hogben said in his book, *On the Green*: "It seems that the most reticent of men on other subjects no sooner takes to golf than eloquence descends upon him."

These quotations, arranged by subject, are taken from a variety of sources: magazines, newspapers, radio, television, books, and the presstent; they are, in effect, chip shots, the chip shot being defined by the *Encyclopedia of Golf* as "a short approach." We hope with these chip shots to encourage the reader to explore the richness of golf literature, an area that golf historian Herbert Warren Wind says ". . . far surpasses any other game's for sheer quantity," and of which author George Plimpton says, "No other sport can offer such fine reading."

For their own contribution, we would like to thank Nelson Cullenward, Lynne Dust, Donna Pinnick, Hank Pollex, Paul Ragghianti, Melinda Shier-Halverson and Joseph Zablocki.

We hope you enjoy the words of golf.

Bob Chieger and Pat Sullivan
June, 1985

Inside Golf

1. Amateurs and Duffers

Out on the course each morning you could see representatives of every nightmare style that was ever invented. There was the man who seemed to be attempting to deceive his ball and lull it into a false security by looking away from it and then making a lightning slash in the apparent hope of catching it off its guard.

P. G. Wodehouse
"The Heart of a Goof," 1923

Even in foursomes where fifty yards is reckoned a good shot somebody must be away.

P. G. Wodehouse
"Chester Forgets Himself," 1923

I won't try to describe A.R.'s game, beyond saying the way he played it would have taken him three years of solid practice to work up to where he could be called a duffer.

Paul Gallico
Golf Is a Nice Friendly Game, 1942

If I were a man I wouldn't have a half a dozen Tom Collinses before going out to play golf, then let profanity substitute for proficiency on the golf course.

Patty Berg
Ladies' Home Journal, 1945

Under an assumed name.

Dutch Harrison, his advice to a hacker on how to play a shot during a pro-am

As I burst into the clubhouse to tell everyone, news came that Lindbergh had flown the Atlantic. Guess who's remembered?

Herb Graffis, golf editor, on his first ace, 1950

Give me golf clubs, the fresh air and a beautiful partner and you can keep my golf clubs and the fresh air.

Jack Benny

Every time I have the urge to play golf I lie down until the urge passes.

Sam Levenson, humorist

A golfer might as well turn in his clubs if he can't find some excuse for his own duffery.

Milton Gross
Eighteen Holes in My Head, 1959

The cross-handed grip is used principally by left-handed golfers who have purchased right-handed clubs by mistake (or vice-versa) and is too special for discussion here.

Rex Lardner
Out of the Bunker and Into the Trees, 1960

This will give the duffers a bit of heart.

Arnold Palmer, as he took a twelve on the final hole of the Los Angeles Open, 1961

Any golfer serious enough about his game to want to break 120 must learn to stop worrying about the last ten or twenty missed strokes.

Stephen Baker
How to Play Golf in the Low 120's, 1962

Nothing goes down slower than a golf handicap.
Bobby Nichols
Never Say Never, 1965

If you pick up a golfer and hold it close to your ear, like a
conch shell, and listen—you will hear an alibi.
Fred Beck
89 Years in a Sand Trap, 1965

The average golfer doesn't play golf. He attacks it.
Jackie Burke

Your financial cost can best be figured out when you realize
that if you were to devote the same time and energy to business instead of golf, you would be a millionaire in approximately six weeks.
Buddy Hackett
The Truth About Golf and Other Lies, 1968

I am the world's foremost master at the topped shot. Not
everyone can learn to play this delicate little line drive around
the green with finesse.
Jim Murray
The Sporting World of Jim Murray, 1968

You were hitting some shots out there that weren't making any
noise.
**Dave Marr, to George Plimpton at the Bing Crosby
National Pro-Am**

The biggest liar in the world is the golfer who claims that he
plays the game merely for exercise.
Tommy Bolt
How to Keep Your Temper on the Golf Course, 1969

I had always suspected that trying to play golf in the company of big-time pros and a gallery would be something like walking naked into choir practice.

>   **Dan Jenkins, on pro-ams**
>   *The Dogged Victims of Inexorable Fate,* 1970

Mulligan: Invented by an Irishman who wanted to hit one more twenty-yard grounder.

>   **Jim Bishop, syndicated column, 1970**

Like all Saturday foursomes it is in difficulties. One of the patients is zigzagging about the fairway like a liner pursued by submarines.

>   **P. G. Wodehouse**
>   *P. G. Wodehouse on Golf,* 1973

I have three-putted in forty countries.

>   **Fred Corcoran, former PGA executive director**
>   *Golf Digest,* 1977

How about that guy? He gives me a stroke a side and I still have to shoot a sixty-eight to beat him. The lousy sandbagger.

>   **Bob Hope**

The loudest sound you hear on the golf course is the guy jangling coins to distract the player he bets against.

>   **Jim Murray, *Los Angeles Times* sports columnist**

Bob Newhart to Suzanne Pleshette: It was a great dude ranch. I shot an eighty-three.

>   **"The Bob Newhart Show," NBC-TV, 1980**

I may be the only golfer never to have broken a single putter, if you don't count the one I twisted into a loop and threw into a bush.

Thomas Boswell, sportswriter
Golf Digest, 1980

As of this writing, there are approximately 2,450 reasons why a person hits a rotten shot, and more are being discovered every day.

Jay Cronley
Playboy, 1981

Hell is standing on the most beautiful golf course that's ever been made and not having a set of clubs.

Jim Meyers, radio station general manager
San Francisco Chronicle, 1982

The flags on the greens ought to be at half-staff.

Al Malatesta, amateur golfer, on his game
San Francisco Examiner, 1982

If I died . . . it meant I couldn't play golf. No way was I giving up golf, so I gave up drinking.

Bob Hope
Los Angeles Times, 1982

I call him the PGA hit man. But it's wonderful being able to get back some of that money I gave to the government.

Bob Hope, on President Gerald R. Ford
San Jose Mercury News, 1982

Bob says I have made golf a combat and contact sport.

Gerald R. Ford, on Bob Hope
People, 1983

And the name that is synonomous with Ford—Fore!
Vin Scully
"Bob Hope Classic," NBC-TV, 1984

My tournament lineup would include . . . anyone who never finished a par-five hole with the same ball he started it with.
Jim Murray
Los Angeles Times, 1983

If you used these pin placements on a Saturday afternoon with municipal players, they'd be out here two weeks.
Lee Trevino
"Isuzu-Andy Williams San Diego Open," NBC-TV, 1983

When you're looking at the scores, start at the bottom.
Frank Dill, San Francisco radio personality, playing in the Bing Crosby National Pro-Am, 1983

Thinking you are going to win the Crosby Pro-Am with a high handicap makes as much sense as leaving the porch light on for Jimmy Hoffa.
Phil Harris
"Bing Crosby National Pro-Am," CBS-TV, 1983

2. Brains and Flakes

Never saw one who was worth a damn.
Harry Vardon, asked about left-handed golfers, 1900

God must watch over left-handers, because nobody else does.
Furman Bisher, *Atlanta Journal* sports columnist, 1984

How in the world did they ever get that? I never been to New York in my life.

Sam Snead, when shown a picture of himself in the New York papers after winning the Oakland Open, 1937

I sure am glad we don't have to play in the shade.

Walter Hagen, when told at a match in Florida that it was 105 degrees in the shade, 1926

The trick is to know when that one time is about to happen.

Walter Hagen, after betting ten dollars on a hole-in-one, a one in 100,000 shot, and making it

Typically, for a man who might spend three-quarters of an hour shaving, The Haig spent more than six years of his retirement writing his autobiography, five of which were devoted to searching for just the right title.

Charles Price
The World of Golf, 1962

What are you trying to do, man? You had ten birdies today. Why, the officials are still inside talking about it. They're thinking of putting a limit on you.

Jimmy Demaret, when he saw Ben Hogan practicing after Hogan shot a record sixty-four in the Rochester Open, 1941

Not necessarily. It simply seems to require more skill than I have at the moment.

Ben Hogan, when asked if the twelfth hole at Augusta was impossible

What did he go out in?

Sam Snead, upon hearing on election day that Thomas Dewey was leading, 1948

Have you ever noticed that most of the young guys who come out here are pretty big? Most of them are built like a truck driver. And did you notice they can all putt? Well, the trouble with you is, you're built like a hairdresser and you've got a touch like a truck driver.

Clayton Heafner, to Charles Price, 1948

What are you gonna do, build a bonfire?

George Low, club professional, when a member dipped in for tees

Excuse me, madam, would you mind either standing back or closing your mouth—I've lost four balls already.

Ted Ray, comedian, to a spectator at a charity match in Scotland, 1952

Hey, Lindbergh got eight days of confetti for less than this.

Jimmy Demaret, on a bumpy flight to Japan for the World Cup

The valleys are so narrow that the dogs have to wag their tails up and down.

Sam Snead, on his birthplace in the mountains of Virginia
The Education of a Golfer, 1962

In February 1949, Ben Hogan had his famous motor accident —it is an interesting reflection that had he been wearing a seat belt at the time he would now have been dead some sixteen years.

Henry Longhurst
"Highlights of the Ryder Cup," 1965

The University of Houston, better known as the "University of Golf," where, the gag goes, the entrance requirements are a sixty-four on an accredited course and a sound short game.
                                    Jim Murray
                                    The Best of Jim Murray, 1965

Fifteen years ago Houston had the three best teams in the country—the five guys that made it and the ten that missed it.
                        Mike Holder, Oklahoma State golf coach
                        Sports Illustrated, 1984

Three of the happiest years of my life were in the second grade.
                    Joe Kirkwood, Australian-born professional, 1967

Hey, Arnie, how 'bout letting us play through.
                    Chi Chi Rodriguez, to Arnold Palmer and his Army
                    at The Masters, 1970

Where the ##%&+&@ are the marshalls!
                    Tommy Bolt, as deer twice ran across the fairway
                    at the Bing Crosby National Pro-Am, 1970

My family was so poor they couldn't afford any kids. The lady next door had me.
                                    Lee Trevino
                                    Sports Illustrated, 1971

If you don't shut up, I'm going to tell where you swam across the border.
                    Doug Sanders, to Lee Trevino at The Masters

The hardest thing was being young and coming onto the tour right out of high school and a very close home environment. I think the thing I miss most is my mother's homemade soup.

Amy Alcott, age twenty-one
New York Times, 1977

I was born in the southeastern part of Oklahoma. Ever hear of Idabel? . . . It was so far back in the sticks, they had to pipe daylight in there.

Tommy Bolt
Golf Digest, 1977

I only use glasses when I want to see. I even keep them close to my bed so I can see my dreams.

Tom Kite
Golf Digest, 1978

Did you ever smell your golf bag after you carried a tuna sandwich around in the hot sun?

Al Geiberger, on why he chose peanut butter
Golf Digest, 1978

When I left the course after a round this year, a lady told me that my biorhythms were off. I told her my golf game was off.

Jack Nicklaus
Golf Digest, 1978

I like cowboy-and-Indian books. I read that night until I forgot about my problems and started worrying about the Indians.

Seve Ballesteros, at the British Open, 1979

2. Brains and Flakes 13

I started in engineering and switched to business for my major. If I had stayed for my junior year, I'd have had to switch to basket weaving. It was getting tough.

Nancy Lopez
Golf Digest, 1979

I'm playing better now than I ever have in my career. I don't know what's happened, but I'm not going to search for the answer.

Raymond Floyd, after winning the Doral-Eastern Open, 1981

On the 18th hole, a par 4, I first thought of using my 4-wood on my second shot. But, you see, my 4-wood is actually a 5-wood and my 3-wood is actually a 4-wood. Realizing my 4-wood would wind up short—that's actually my 5-wood—I went instead to my 3-wood, actually my 4-wood. So, the shot put me closer to the hole and I could 2-putt. I used my head. For a Puerto Rican, that's pretty good thinking.

Chi Chi Rodriguez
San Jose Mercury News, 1981

Too frequently their idea of great art is a painting of the Quarry Hole at Merion. Their literature seems to consist of the Rules of Golf or Ben Hogan's fundamentals.

Art Spander, on professional golfers
Golf Magazine, 1981

There's a full moon, and I'll tell you I've been affected. I'm pulling energy from all over the world. Friends from all over, from Tokyo, California, everywhere, are pulling for me. And I'm pulling in the vibes.

Muffin Spencer-Devlin
The Sporting News, 1982

I never did see the sense in keeping my head down. The only reason I play golf at all is to see where the ball goes.

Charles Price
Golfer-At-Large, 1982

I thought you had to be dead to win that.

JoAnne Carner, on winning the Bob Jones Award for sportsmanship
Sports Illustrated, 1982

It's this way. I'd start for my economics class and wind up at a driving range.

Roger Maltbie, on why he didn't finish college
Golf Magazine, 1982

By the time I was five I was out in the fields, too. I thought hard work was just how life was. I was twenty-one years old before I knew Manual Labor wasn't a Mexican.

Lee Trevino
They Call Me Super Mex, 1982

That ball had more bite on it than any other during the round.

J.C. Snead, as a dog grabbed his ball at the U.S. Open
San Francisco Examiner, 1982

Why do I love kids so much? Because I was never a kid myself. I was too poor to be a child, so I never really had a childhood. The biggest present I ever got was a marble.

Chi Chi Rodriguez
Golf Digest, 1983

I'm really fifteen years younger than my birth certificate shows. In Virginia, we don't count the years you go barefoot.

Sam Snead
Golf Magazine, 1983

Is that right? How long are decades nowadays?
**Sam Snead, on being told he has won tournaments in
six different decades**
Sports Illustrated, 1983

I love to sweat and heave and breathe and hurt and burn and
get dirty. . . . There's something good about getting all dirty
and grimy and nasty and then showering; you feel twice as
clean.

Jan Stephenson
Playboy, 1983

It's funny. You need a fantastic memory in this game to remember the great shots, and a very short memory to forget
the bad ones.

Gary McCord, at the Bing Crosby National Pro-Am
Sports Illustrated, 1984

The ultimate accomplishment of my life? That was in 1958
when I got a trophy for perfect attendance in a bowling
league . . . That set the whole precedent of my life.

Gary McCord
San Jose Mercury News, 1984

Do you know what my favorite course was? Cafeteria.

Mac O'Grady
Sports Illustrated, 1984

I don't trust doctors. They are like golfers. Every one has a
different answer to your problem.

Seve Ballesteros
Seve: The Young Champion, 1984

I never had a good bounce. All I ever had were bad ones.

Arnold Palmer
Golf Magazine, 1984

College? I thought it was just somewhere where guys played football. . . . If I'd gone to college, though, I probably wouldn't have liked it. Everybody's too damned serious for me.

Lee Trevino
Golf Magazine, 1984

I didn't need to finish college to know what golf was all about. All you need to know is to hit the ball, find it and hit it again until it disappears into the hole in the ground.

Fuzzy Zoeller
Golf Magazine, 1984

Reporter: What's it like to be Jack Nicklaus' son?
Nicklaus II: I don't know. I've never had anybody else for a father.

Jack Nicklaus II
San Francisco Chronicle, 1984

They're ripping it at the flag—of course I guess that's where the hole is.

Ken Venturi
"Doral-Eastern Open," CBS-TV, 1984

The only people who come to visit us are *lost.*

Bruce Lietzke, on his secluded home in northeastern Oklahoma
Golf Magazine, 1984

In Japan, player who scores hole-in-one while leading tournament always lose. It's proven jinx.

Ayako Okamoto
PGA Magazine, 1984

Reporter: How hot is it out there on the course?
Zoeller: It's as hot as my first wrist watch.

Fuzzy Zoeller, 1984

3. Caddies

The player may experiment about his swing, his grip, his stance. It is only when he begins asking his caddie's advice that he is getting on dangerous ground.

> **Sir Walter Simpson**
> *The Art of Golf*, 1887

Vardon: What on earth shall I take now?
Caddie: Well, sir, I'd recommend the 4:05 train.

> **Harry Vardon, playing poorly and uncertain about his club selection**

I have been playing golf three hundred and seventy-five (expletive deleted) years and after all that time I reach the day where I ask a twenty-five-year-old caddie what club to use.

> **Bobby Cruickshank, after a double bogey at the U.S. Open, 1924**

There were three things in the world that he held in the smallest esteem—slugs, poets, and caddies with hiccups.

> **P. G. Wodehouse**
> "Rodney Fails to Qualify," 1924

I think it is slightly straight, Mr. Faulkner.

> **Mad Mac, caddie, advising Britisher Max Faulkner on a putt**

When I ask you what kind of club to use, look the other way and don't answer.

> **Sam Snead, to his caddie before a tough match**

I've been caddying for him for ten years and he's never had a bad lie yet.

Skeets, caddie for Bob Hope, c. 1950s

I asked [my caddie] what had been so important to require a phone call after the starter had summoned us to the tee. "I wanted to call the wife to tell her not to wait for dinner," he said wistfully, "and to kiss the kids goodnight for me."

Milton Gross
Eighteen Holes in My Head, 1959

Why ask me? You've asked me two times already and paid no attention to what I said. Pick your own club.

Dow Finsterwald's caddie, at the U.S. Open, 1960

We work as a team—I hand him the clubs and he makes the shots.

Nathaniel (Ironman) Avery, Arnold Palmer's caddie

When Mr. Palmer's gettin' ready to make his move, he jerks at that glove, pulls up his britches and starts walkin' fast. When he do that, everybody better watch out. He gonna stampede anything that gets in his way.

Nathaniel (Ironman) Avery, at The Masters, 1962

Sarazen: I'm sorry, Joe. I went to church last Sunday and I prayed.
Caddie: Well, boss, I don't know what you folks pray about when you go to church, but when I go to church I keep my head down.

Gene Sarazen and caddie, at qualifying for the U.S. Open
Daily Telegraph (London), 1963

Shor, after shooting a 211: What should I give the caddie?
Gleason: Your golf clubs.

Toots Shor and Jackie Gleason

Never let him tell you anything more than how deep the hole
is and what time it is.

Jim Murray, on caddies
The Sporting World of Jim Murray, 1968

I am going to win so much money this year my caddie will
make the top twenty money-winners' list.

Lee Trevino
Sports Illustrated, 1973

If a caddie can help you, then you don't know how to play
golf.

Dan Jenkins
Dead Solid Perfect, 1974

One caddie was explaining why he couldn't loan out any
more money. "I sent my Crosby check to my wife, my In-
verrary check to my grandmother, my Citrus check to my girl
friend, and I already bet this one on the Boston Celtics."

Dan Gleason
The Great, The Grand and the Also-Ran, 1976

Cart paths at Pebble Beach? What next? AstroTurf greens at
St. Andrews?

Art Spander
Golf Digest, 1977

We just prayin' we're both still out here when Roy's pants
come back in style.

Lee Trevino, on a caddie
Golf Digest, 1978

My game is so bad I gotta hire three caddies—one to walk the left rough, one for the right rough, and one down the middle. And the one in the middle doesn't have much to do.

Dave Hill
Golf Digest, 1979

My own experience as a caddie imparted lasting knowledge to me in only two areas—sex and poker.

Larry Sheehan
Great Golf Humor from Golf Digest, 1979

He'd rather go to the beach. I think the only reason he puts up with caddying is because he has to eat. Angelo has basically been retired since he was twenty-one.

Jack Nicklaus, on his caddie Angelo Argea, 1979

There's something haunting about getting up at dawn and walking a golf course, checking pin placements. It's easy to lose track of reality.

Ernest (Creamy) Carolan, caddie
Sports Illustrated, 1981

My caddie said today on the thirteenth hole, "Hit the tee shot over the third hump." I did. We went out and the ball was fifteen yards into waist-high grass. I said, "What happened?" "Wrong hump, governor," he apologized.

Ray Floyd, at the British Open
Washington Post, 1981

I don't know why that putt hung on the edge. I'm a clean liver. It must be my caddie.

JoAnne Carner
Golf Digest, 1981

Caddies are a breed of their own. If you shoot 66, they say, "Man, *we* shot sixty-six!" But go out and shoot 77 and they say, "Hell, *he* shot seventy-seven!"

Lee Trevino
They Call Me Super Mex, 1982

Don't worry about it. Everybody has bad days. The chairman of the board has bad days. Multimillionaires have bad days. The Pope has bad days.

Herman Mitchell, caddie, consoling Lee Trevino, 1982

You get either the youngest caddie or the oldest golf car— and neither works.

Richard Haskell, Massachusetts Golf Association executive director
Golf Digest, 1982

He told me just to keep the ball low.

Chi Chi Rodriguez, putting advice from his caddie
The Sporting News, 1982

At Eldorado I once gave the guy a $5 bill and he said, "Thanks for the ball marker."

Bob Hope, tipping his caddie
Golf Digest, 1983

I was lying 10 and had a 35-foot putt. I whispered over my shoulder, "How does this one break?" And he said, "Who cares?" That's the greatest line from a caddie I ever heard.

Jack Lemmon, playing the Bing Crosby National Pro-Am
San Jose Mercury News, 1983

When he gets the ball into a tough place, that's when he's most relaxed. I think it's because he has so much experience at it.

Don Christopher, caddie for Jack Lemmon
San Jose Mercury News, 1983

Once when I'd been in a lot of bunkers, my caddie told me he was getting blisters from raking so much.

JoAnne Carner
San Francisco Examiner, 1983

My caddie and I had a difference of opinion about which way the putt broke. He was wrong, but I'm the one who had to take the score.

Hale Irwin
San Jose Mercury News, 1984

He looks like he had his hair done in a pet shop.

Dave Marr, on a caddie
"British Open," ABC-TV, 1984

The only time I talk on a golf course is to my caddie—and only then to complain.

Seve Ballesteros
Golf World, 1984

4. Character and the Mind

If profanity had an influence on the flight of the ball, the game would be played far better than it is.

Horace G. Hutchinson
Hints on the Game of Golf, 1886

Golf has some drawbacks. It is possible by too much of it to destroy the mind; a man with a Roman nose and a high forehead may play away his profile.

Sir Walter Simpson
The Art of Golf, 1887

After taking the stance, it is too late to worry. The only thing to do then is to hit the ball.

Bobby Jones
Vanity Fair, 1929

I'm going to miss at least seven shots in every eighteen holes, so if I'm going to be angry, I might as well start right on the first tee.

Walter Hagen

Give me a man with big hands, big feet and no brains and I will make a golfer out of him.

Walter Hagen

I say this without any reservations whatsoever. It is impossible to outplay an opponent you can't out-think.

Lawson Little, American professional

In a gin'ral way, all I can say about it is that it's a kind iv game iv ball that ye play with ye'er own worst inimy, which is ye'ersilf.

Finley Peter Dunne, American humorist

Good golfing temperament falls between taking it with a grin or shrug and throwing a fit.

Sam Snead

Golf is a funny game. It's done much for health, and at the same time has ruined people by robbing them of their peace of mind. Look at me, I'm the healthiest idiot in the world.

Bob Hope

The most advanced medical brains in the universe have yet to discover a way for a man to relax himself, and looking at a golf ball is not the cure.

Milton Gross
Eighteen Holes in My Head, 1959

The most exquisitely satisfying act in the world of golf is that of throwing a club. The full backswing, the delayed wrist action, the flowing follow-through, followed by that unique whirring sound, reminiscent only of a passing flock of starlings, are without parallel in sport.

Henry Longhurst
"✺✺✺✺✺✺✺✺✺✺!", 1965

I've thrown or broken a few clubs in my day. In fact, I guess at one time or another I probably held distance records for every club in the bag.

Tommy Bolt
How to Keep Your Temper on the Golf Course, 1969

Why, during those early days Palmer was on tour, he threw them. I have to say that he was the very worst golf-club thrower I have ever seen. He had to learn to play well, he'd have never made it as a thrower.

Tommy Bolt
The Hole Truth, 1971

About the only thing left for me is acupuncture—in the brain.

**George Archer, walking off the final green at the
Hawaiian Open**
Golf Magazine, 1974

I tell the lady scorekeepers that if they can hear me cuss, they're standing too close. They've got to realize they're not at a church social.

Dave Hill, 1975

I buried a few in the ground, you know. It took two men to get one of them out.

Dave Hill
Teed Off, 1977

Golf is a game of expletives not deleted.

Dr. Irving A. Gladstone
Confessions of a Golf Duffer, 1977

I looked around for any generals or corporation presidents I might recognize in the throng, reached for my cigarettes, dropped them, picked them up, stuck one in my ear and set fire to my nose.

Dan Jenkins, playing a pro-am
Golf Digest, 1979

Like one's own children, golf has an uncanny way of endearing itself to us while at the same time evoking every weakness of mind and character, no matter how well hidden.

W. Timothy Gallwey
The Inner Game of Golf, 1979

Let's face it, ninety-five percent of this game is mental. A guy plays lousy golf, he doesn't need a pro, he needs a shrink.

Tom Murphy, touring professional

As every golfer knows, no one ever lost his mind over one shot. It is rather the gradual process of shot-after-shot watching your score go to tatters, . . . knowing that you have found a different way to bogey each one.

Thomas Boswell
Golf Digest, 1980

When I play my best golf, I feel as if I'm in a fog, . . . standing back watching the earth in orbit with a golf club in your hands.

Mickey Wright
Golf Digest, 1981

Your ego is everything. And if you don't get that pumped up regularly, you can't last.

Dave Marr

To succeed at anything, you must have a huge ego. I'm not talking about confidence. Confidence is self-assurance for a reason. Ego is self-assurance for no good reason.

Frank Beard
Golf Magazine, 1981

When you reflect on the combination of characteristics that golf demands of those who would presume to play it, it is not surprising that golf has never had a truly great player who was not also a person of extraordinary character.

Frank D. (Sandy) Tatum, Jr.
The U.S. Open Book, 1982

Golf is a nonviolent game played violently from within.

Bob Toski
Golf Digest, 1982

I actually feel that the unconscious mind has much better control than the conscious mind. The mind uses words, and the muscles don't understand English.

W. Timothy Gallwey
Golf Magazine, 1982

Every day I try to tell myself this is going to be fun today. I try to put myself in a great frame of mind before I go out—then I screw it up with the first shot.

Johnny Miller
Golf Magazine, 1984

It was stupid. I learned a lesson. When you have a fight with a club, the club always wins.

Patti Hayes, on kicking her club and injuring her foot at the Samaritan Turquoise Classic, 1984

This is the hardest game in the world, believe me. There is no way a golfer can think he is really something, because that's when the game gets you.

Ben Crenshaw
San Jose Mercury News, 1984

I would like to knock it on every green and two-putt, but that's not my style of play or my style of living.

Muffin Spencer-Devlin
Seattle Times, 1984

I don't have any particular hang-ups about superstitions. I did try them all, but they didn't work.

Kathy Whitworth, after her eighty-sixth career win, Safeco Classic, 1984

If you're stupid enough to whiff, you should be smart enough to forget it.

> **Arnold Palmer, at the U.S. Senior Open**
> *Sports Illustrated,* 1984

5. Celebrities

The fun you get from golf is in direct ratio to the effort you don't put into it.

> **Bob Allen, comedian, 1950**

I can't say for sure, but I'd like to have that much footage along Wilshire Boulevard.

> **Phil Harris, when asked if his birdie putt really traveled ninety feet, at the Bing Crosby National Pro-Am, 1951**

Obviously she has seen you tee off before and knows that the safest place to be when you play is right down the middle.

> **Jackie Gleason, to writer Milton Gross when a deer wouldn't leave the fairway**

Who plays golf anymore? I've gone in for gambling now. At the tables I only lose my money. On the course I lose my mind.

> **Jackie Miles, comic**

He would rather win a golf match than an Oscar.

> **Bing Crosby, on Bob Hope**
> New York *Herald Tribune,* 1953

Bing Crosby invented the pipe, the shirt worn outside the pants, the cocked hat. He is so rich even his caddies subscribe to *Fortune*.

Bob Hope

Hope invented the nonbody turn, the interlocking grip on a money clip, the fast backswing and a good short game—off the tee.

Bing Crosby

Two of my favorites out there . . . are comedian Bing Crosby and singer Bob Hope. Or is it the other way around? I always forget which one thinks he's funny and which one thinks he can sing.

Jimmy Demaret
My Partner, Ben Hogan, 1954

The hardest shot is a mashie at ninety yards from the green, where the ball has to be played against an oak tree, bounces back into a sandtrap, hits a stone, bounces on the green and then rolls into the cup. That shot is so difficult I have only made it once.

Zeppo Marx

I find it to be the hole-in-one.
Groucho Marx, when asked about the most difficult shot

And now here's Jack Lemmon, about to hit that all-important eighth shot.
Jim McKay, on Lemmon playing the fourteenth hole at Pebble Beach
"Bing Crosby National Pro-Am," ABC-TV, 1959

Jack's getting more footage here today than he had in his last three films.

Bing Crosby
"Bing Crosby National Pro-Am," ABC-TV, 1959

I would rather play Hamlet with no rehearsal than play golf on television.

Jack Lemmon

Jack Lemmon has been in more bunkers than Eva Braun.

Phil Harris

Phil is the only man I know who keeps his left arm straight all day, and bent all night.

Paul Hahn, trickshot golfer, on Phil Harris

Phil can drink more than Dean Martin with one lip tied behind his back.

Jimmy Demaret, on Phil Harris

I'm not a drunk. A drunk is a guy with yellow tennis shoes and a rusty zipper.

Phil Harris

Hope: Okay, what's wrong with my game?
Palmer: If you're talking about golf, that's *not* your game.
Arnold Palmer and Bob Hope
"Chrysler Presents a Bob Hope Special," NBC-TV, 1963

My subject tonight will be golf. At least we have that in common, Bob. I play the game, too. I don't have to tell you what my handicap is—you told me when I tried to join your club.
Flip Wilson, to Bob Hope at a celebrity roast

My handicap is that I am a one-eyed Negro.

Sammy Davis, Jr.

What a foolish thing for her to do. Now she'll have to play all her drives off the back tees.

Bing Crosby, on hearing of a sex-change operation

Murray: Have I got a shot to the green?
Caddie: Mr. Murray, I'd say you have several shots to the green.

Jan Murray, comic

I think I've got the idea now.

Hoagy Carmichael, composer, after an ace at Pebble Beach

Be funny on a golf course? Do I kid my best friend's mother about her heart condition?

Phil Silvers, comedian

One day, I called Dean Martin and said, "Dean, do you want to play golf?" And he said, "Sorry, Buddy, we already have three."

Buddy Hackett
The Truth About Golf and Other Lies, 1968

He played so poorly [in the 1967 Bing Crosby National Pro-Am] that his singing teacher quit him, he was cancelled out of $160,000 worth of bookings and before he got back to the hotel at Carmel, they gave his room away to a better player.

Buddy Hackett, on Robert Goulet
The Truth About Golf and Other Lies, 1968

Vic Damone would be a fine player, but he's too busy looking in the grass to see if he can find a mirror.

Don Rickles

Johnny Carson plays fantastic golf on television when he stands in front of the camera with his funny little swing. On the golf course, the man has trouble walking against the wind.

Don Rickles

I never pray on the golf course. Actually, the Lord answers my prayers everywhere except on the course.

Rev. Billy Graham
Golf Magazine, 1970

How could a guy who won the West, recaptured Bataan and won the battle of Iwo Jima let himself be defeated by a little hole in the ground?

James Edward Grant, screenwriter, on John Wayne
giving up golf
Golf Digest, 1973

There is a certain romance in futility pursued. A golfer always loses on the golf course.

Efrem Zimbalist, Jr., actor

Not only are three-putt greens probable. At times they're an achievement.

Charley Pride, country singer, 1978

I only see Charley when we get to the greens. Charley hits some good woods—most of them are trees.

Glen Campbell, on playing with Pride

I am a victim of circumference. When I stand close enough to the ball to reach it, I can't see it. When I see it, I can't reach it.

Toots Shor, restaurateur

This is the greatest. What a way to relax! Before this I used to get no exercise except for the walk from the bar to the men's room in Toots Shor's.

Jackie Gleason

You know you're not going to wind up with anything but grief, pal, but you can't resist the impulse.

Jackie Gleason, comparing golf to an unpromising woman
Golf Digest, 1977

He's the only man I know who plays thirty-six holes a day without ever seeing the ball. . . . He donated a sweater to charity and now there's a family of refugees living in it.

Bob Hope, on Jackie Gleason
Golf Digest, 1981

I love to play with Andy, but he can be very distracting. Have you ever tried to pitch over a water hazard while your partner is humming "Moon River"?

Bob Hope, on Andy Williams
Golf Digest, 1981

I do a lot of humming out on the course. I tend to stick with one song. . . . I shot a sixty-six to "Moon River."

Jack Nicklaus

Par is anything you want it to be. For instance, this hole here is a par forty-seven. And yesterday I birdied the sucker.

Willie Nelson, country singer, on the course he purchased near Austin, Texas, 1981

If that's true, I'm the first dead man to make six double bogeys on the back nine on the day of his funeral.

> **Victor Mature, actor, when his death was erroneously reported on radio**
> *Golf Digest*, 1982

If this was a prize fight, they'd stop it.

> **Bob Hope, on his golf game**
> *San Jose Mercury News*, 1982

The toughest part about matches with Crosby was collecting.

> **Bob Hope**
> *Golf Magazine*, 1983

Telly Savalas, struggling under an eighteen handicap, now needs a three ax to get out of this trouble.

> **Vin Scully**
> "Bob Hope Classic," NBC-TV, 1984

6. Course Design and Places

If I had my way, I'd never let the sand be raked. Instead, I'd run a herd of elephants through them every morning.

> **Charles Blair Macdonald, American course architect**

This guy was so rugged in his thinking that he probably wore his tweed knickerbockers without any underwear.

> **Charles Price, on Macdonald**
> *Golf Magazine*, 1974

A golf course is the epitome of all that is purely transitory in the universe, a space not to dwell in, but to get over as quickly as possible.

Jean Giraudoux
The Enchanted, 1933

Alaska would be an ideal place for courses—mighty few trees and damn few ladies' foursomes.

Rex Lardner
Out of the Bunker and Into the Trees, 1960

A great golf hole is one which puts a question mark into the player's mind when he arrives on the tee to play it.

Mackenzie Ross, British course architect

Anyone who criticizes a golf course is like a person invited to a house for dinner who, on leaving, tells the host that the food was lousy.

Gary Player

Golf in and around Los Angeles tends to be—like the rest of the landscape—unreal, . . . part Royal and Ancient, part Disneyland. The Good Ship Lollipop with four-irons.

Jim Murray
"Golf in Disneyland," 1973

Every hole should be a demanding par and a comfortable bogey.

Robert Trent Jones, American course architect
Golf Magazine, 1976

"The man who hates golfers" is what they call me. They couldn't be more wrong. I design holes that are fun to play.

Robert Trent Jones

Saw a course you'd really like, Trent. On the first tee you drop the ball over your left shoulder.

Jimmy Demaret

The real trick of golf course architecture is to lure the golfer into a false sense of security.

Peter Dye
Golf Digest, 1979

Pebble Beach is so exclusive that even the Samaritans have an unlisted number.

Peter Dobereiner
National Amateur Championship program, 1981

That's how architects make their money, always going back to fix what they don't do right in the first place.

Lee Trevino
Golf Digest, 1981

All truly great golf courses have an almost supernatural finishing hole, by way of separating the chokers from the strokers.

Charles Price
Golf Magazine, 1981

There's no such thing as a bad course. Courses are like people —each course has its own personality. You have to challenge each one as it comes along.

Barbara Mizrahie
Golf Digest, 1982

Dye's true hallmark is the use of railroad ties, telephone poles or planking to shore up greens, sand traps and the banks of water hazards. He uses so much wood that one of his courses may be the first ever to burn down.

Barry McDermott, on architect Peter Dye
Sports Illustrated, 1982

There was no doubt a few professionals watching who were hoping that the water was ten feet deep and neither could swim. Especially Dye.

Ron Coffman, when Jerry Pate threw Peter Dye in the water at the Tournament Players Championship
Golf World, 1982

Are you sure he's really building a golf course out here? He's already spent $1.5 million and I don't have anything that looks like a golf course.

Joe Walser, president of Oak Tree, on Peter Dye
Golf Digest, 1983

There is no denying that golf has put Hilton Head Island on the map. After all, how many homes can you build around a tennis court?

Charles Price, golf writer

It's pretty, but too golfy.

Hollis Stacy, on Hilton Head Island
San Francisco Examiner, 1983

There are no straight lines on my courses. The good Lord never drew a straight line.

Jack Nicklaus
Golf Digest, 1983

If I were designing one for myself, there'd be a dogleg right on every hole and the first hole wouldn't count. That would be a warm-up hole.

Lee Trevino
Golf Digest, 1983

Some players would complain if they were playing on Dolly Parton's bedspread.

Jimmy Demaret
Golf Magazine, 1983

Great golf courses should have at least one silly hole.
                              Frank Hannigan, USGA director

It is easier to tell a man that there's something wrong with his wife and child than with his golf course.
                              Frank Hannigan
                              Chicago Tribune, 1984

We come from the same backgrounds, more or less, where growing up next to a golf course didn't mean a 10,000-square foot house and gold faucets in the bathrooms.
                              Lee Trevino, on Seve Ballesteros, 1984

You can treat them [the flowers] as a water hazard and drop your ball to one side. Otherwise, you can try to play it out. However, if you do, you never will be permitted to play SentryWorld again.
                              Robert Trent Jones, on his new course in Wisconsin
                              Golf Digest, 1984

Every course needs a hole that puckers your rear end.
                              Johnny Miller, on the seventeenth at the TPC
                              at Sawgrass
                              "Tournament Players Championship," CBS-TV, 1984

7. The Courses

Augusta National Golf Club, Augusta, Georgia

There isn't a hole out there that can't be birdied if you just think. But there isn't one that can't be double-bogeyed if you stop thinking.
                              Bobby Jones

The greens *are* the course. . . . They are faster than a fart in a hot skillet.

Dave Hill
Teed Off, 1977

The only difference is at Augusta the divots tear loose on dotted lines.

John Updike
"Thirteen Ways of Looking at The Masters," 1980

We could make them [the greens] so slick we'd have to furnish ice skates on the first tee.

Hord Hardin, Augusta National chairman
Golf Digest, 1981

Amen Corner looks like something that fell from heaven, but it plays like something straight out of hell.

Gary Van Sickle
Milwaukee Journal, 1981

They say position is required at Augusta and it's true. Put it 320 yards from where you're standing and you're perfect.

Howard Twitty, on the need for length
Golf Magazine, 1983

There is a saying around north Georgia that the Augusta National Golf Club is the closest thing to heaven for a golfer —and it's just about as hard to get into.

Joe Geshwiler
San Francisco Examiner, 1983

I kept telling Tom, "Let's go ahead and hit before they suspend play." That's one hole you don't want to wake up to.

Mark Lye, to Tom Kite on the par-three twelfth hole, 1984

Bel-Air Golf Club, Los Angeles, California

W.C. Fields was fond of playing the course sideways with his pal, Oliver Hardy. He liked being in the trees where he could drink without scandalizing the natives.

Jim Murray
Golf Digest, 1973

Butler National Golf Club, Oak Brook, Illinois

If the USGA ever got its hands on this course, it would be all over.

Dave Stockton, on the 75.34 course rating, 1975

I used to dream that I could be a waiter in a place like this.

Chi Chi Rodriguez
San Francisco Examiner, 1983

Colonial Country Club, Fort Worth, Texas

Colonial is the halter-top capital of the world.

Tom Brookshier, sports commentator
Texas Monthly, 1977

If you don't like what you see at Colonial, you're too old to be looking.

Norm Alden, Fort Worth disc jockey
Texas Monthly, 1977

The Country Club, Brookline, Massachusetts

To me, the ground here is hallowed. The grass grows greener, the trees bloom better, there is even a warmth to the rocks. I don't know, gentlemen, but somehow or other the sun seems to shine brighter on The Country Club than any other place that I have known.

Francis Ouimet, 1932

Cypress Point Golf Club, Pebble Beach, California

Cypress Point is a dream, . . . so bewilderingly picturesque that it seems to have been the crystallization of the dream of an artist who has been drinking gin and sobering up on absinthe.

O. B. Keeler
The American Golfer, 1929

Cypress Point is the Sistine Chapel of golf.
Frank (Sandy) Tatum, former USGA president

Cypress—what a course that is. It has the looks of Christie Brinkley and the tenderness of Tokyo Rose.
Bob Hope
Golf Magazine, 1983

Cypress Point is so exclusive that it had a membership drive and drove out forty members.

Bob Hope

Firestone Country Club, South Course, Akron, Ohio

The Winner at Firestone? Par!
Golf Magazine, **headline, 1976**

I just can't play this course. It eats my lunch. Firestone's a long-iron course. I'd just as soon pull a rattlesnake out of my bag as a two-iron.

Lee Trevino
Golf Digest, 1979

Harbour Town Golf Club, Hilton Head Island, South Carolina

Harbour Town is so tough even your clubs get tired.
Charles Price
Golf Magazine, 1970

I like to putt the Harbour Town greens. They're so bumpy the gallery can't tell when I have the yips.

Larry Ziegler
Golf Digest, 1978

Hazeltine Golf Club, Chaska, Minnesota

The greens resembled Indian burial mounds more than anything else. And their horses had been buried along with the Indians.

Dave Hill
Teed Off, 1977

Houston Country Club, Houston, Texas

The Houston Country Club has gold dust instead of sand in the traps and the greens are irrigated with oil. It is home base for those hackneyed caricatures, the Texas zillionaire and his lady hung with ice cubes.

Red Smith
"A Hundred and Four Years Old," 1964

Lakeside Country Club, Los Angeles, California

A requirement at Lakeside was that you be able to hold your booze. That was the club of the hard-drinking Irish and the gag, standard for admission, was that you had to be able to kill a fifth in nine holes.

Jim Murray
Los Angeles Times

Los Angeles Country Club, North Course, Los Angeles, California

The eight hundred members comprise the elite of California and legend has it that when one member proposed a movie star for membership once, they not only turned the star down, they threw out the guy who proposed him.

Jim Murray
The Sporting World of Jim Murray, 1968

Medinah Country Club, Number Three, Medinah, Illinois

Golf architects dream about creating such a hole. Players dream about boiling architects in oil.

> **John Marshall, resident pro, on the tough par-three seventeenth hole**

Merion Golf Club, East Course, Ardmore, Pennsylvania

If you hit this green with your second shot, you heave a sigh so deep that it is usually audible a mashie shot away.

> **Robert Trent Jones, on the par-four eleventh hole "Merion"**

I didn't beat Merion. I just compromised with her, like a wife, trying not to let her have her way too often.

> **Lee Trevino, upon winning the U.S. Open, 1971**

That course doesn't even belong in the top 200! They have to grow rough up to your rear end to make it playable for the Open.

> **Sam Snead**
> *Golf Digest*, 1981

Merion wouldn't alter that course for the Second Coming, let alone another golf championship.

> **Charles Price**
> *Golf Magazine*, 1981

Muirfield Village Golf Club, Dublin, Ohio

The Muirfield Village Golf course near Columbus, Ohio, site of last week's tournament, was in such immaculate condition that people would sooner have dropped cigarette butts on their babies' tummies.

> **Dan Jenkins**
> *Sports Illustrated*, 1977

They should have slippers at every hole and pass a rule that you have to take off your shoes before going to the green. They shouldn't be walked on with cleats.

Lee Trevino

There are eighteen bullies out there. You gotta beat 'em up one at a time. You beat up one and here's another bully you got to beat up.

Jack Grout, Muirfield pro-emeritus

Do you realize water comes into play on eighteen shots? That's *eighteen shots!*

Tom Weiskopf

Oakland Hills Country Club, South Course, Birmingham, Michigan

The course is playing the players instead of the players playing the course.

Walter Hagen, at the U.S. Open, 1951

I am glad to have brought this monster to its knees.

Ben Hogan, at the presentation ceremonies of the U.S. Open, 1951

I don't want to make it a lady's course, but I don't want every hole to play like the last one I'm ever going to play.

Lionel Hebert, age fifty-three, at the U.S. Senior Open *San Francisco Examiner*, 1981

Oakmont Country Club, Oakmont, Pennsylvania

You gotta sneak up on these holes. If you clamber and clank up on 'em, they're liable to turn around and bite you.

Sam Snead, 1953

This is a course where good putters worry about their second putt before they hit the first one.

Lew Worsham, Oakmont club professional

You could have combed North Africa with it, and Rommel wouldn't have gotten past Casablanca.

Jimmy Demaret, on the special rake designed for the traps
Golf Magazine, 1983

Onion Creek Golf Club, Austin, Texas

God put it there. All I did was manicure it.

Jimmy Demaret, on his design of the course

Pebble Beach Golf Links, Pebble Beach, California

Pebble Beach is Alcatraz with grass.

Bob Hope, at the Bing Crosby National Pro-Am, 1952

It's like fighting Rocky Marciano, . . . every time you step onto the course, you're a cinch to take a beating.

Jackie Burke, c. 1950s

If you moved Pebble Beach fifty miles inland, no one would have heard of it.

Jimmy Demaret

Pebble Beach is the world's leading argument for indoor golf.

Dan Jenkins, sportswriter

This here is a pivotal hole. If you're five over par when you hit this tee, it's the best place in the world to commit suicide.

Lee Trevino, at the sixth hole
Golf Digest, 1978

The only thing gonna stick around that hole is a dart! Yesterday, I was on in three, off in four! They oughta put one of them miniature windmills on this thing and charge fifty cents to play it.

Lee Trevino, at the fourteenth hole
Golf Digest, 1978

I thought the course treated me rather cruelly. I'm not an obnoxious guy. I don't throw clubs. I'm nice to galleries. I don't deserve some of the things Pebble Beach did to me.

William Israelson, Minnesota professional
San Francisco Examiner, 1982

Pebble is supposed to be as nasty as a cocktail waitress in a dockside cafe.

Art Spander
San Francisco Examiner, 1983

I've heard of unplayable lies, but on the tee?

Bob Hope
Confessions of a Hooker, 1985

This is a bad-ass course.

C. W. Nevius, quoting a caddie
San Francisco Chronicle, 1985

Pinehurst Country Club, Number Two, Pinehurst, North Carolina

The man who doesn't feel emotionally stirred when he golfs at Pinehurst beneath those clear blue skies and with the pine fragrance in his nostrils is one who should be ruled out of golf for life.

Tommy Armour, c. 1960s

Pine Valley Golf Club, Clementon, New Jersey

Tell me, do you chaps actually play this hole—or just photograph it?

> **Eustace Storey, British amateur, on his first look at the second hole, c. 1920s**

It has no rough, in the accepted sense of the term, and no semi-rough. Your ball is either on the fairway, in which case it sits invitingly on a flawless carpet of turf, or it is not. If it is not, you play out sideways till it is.

> **Henry Longhurst**
> *It Was Good While It Lasted*, 1941

In all my travels, I do not think I've seen a more beautiful landscape. This is as thrilling as Versailles or Fontainbleau.

> **Lowell Thomas, American radio news commentator, early 1950s**

"You ever play Pine Valley?" I asked her. *"There's* a tough course! Texas with bunkers!"

> **Rex Lardner**
> *Out of the Bunker and Into the Trees*, 1960

Pine Valley is the shrine of American golf because so many golfers are buried there.

> **Ed Sullivan, American television personality**
> *Philadelphia Bulletin*, 1966

Pine Valley, . . . a weekend in a mental ward.

> **Charles Price**
> *Golf Digest,* 1983

Here is the ultimate expression of sado-masochistic golf, the supreme example of the penal school of architecture. A Philadelphia businessman, George Crump, conceived the idea, possibly during a nightmare.

Peter Dobereiner
Down the Nineteenth Fairway, 1983

Pine Valley has been described as one huge bunker dotted with eighteen greens, eighteen tees and about that many more target areas.

Mike Bryan
Golf Magazine, 1983

Preston Trail Golf Club, Dallas, Texas

If I were ever tempted to get a big head, all I'd have to do is go out and play a round at Preston Trail. Every guy out there can buy and sell me ten times. It puts things in perspective real quick.

Lanny Wadkins
Golf Digest, 1983

Rancho La Costa, Carlsbad, California

Arnold Palmer had no trouble at all taking a twelve there last year although I must say if he played it a little smarter he could have made a nine.

Jim Murray, on the ninth hole
The Sporting World of Jim Murray, 1968

Riviera Golf Club, Pacific Palisades, California

Very nice course. But tell me, where do the members play?
Bobby Jones, c. 1930s

Where's the rest of the fairway? Who stole half of your hole?
Gary Player, upon seeing the narrow par-four eighth hole, c. 1950s

It used to be a hustler's paradise. . . . You could get a bet on the color of the next dog coming up the fairway.

Jim Murray
Golf Digest, 1973

I stayed at the club last year and my room was so clean, I didn't even want to take a shower.

Lee Trevino
USA Today, 1984

Sawgrass Golf Club, Ponte Vedra Beach, Florida

This is the first time I ever withdrew while my ball was still airborne.

Cesar Sanudo, walking off the course after hitting three balls in the water on the ninth hole at the Tournament Players Championship, 1977

We call him [the alligator] Mr. Sawgrass, or sometimes Sir. But like everyone else here he doesn't spend a great deal of time on the fairways.

Jim Blanks, Sawgrass associate professional
Golf Digest, 1977

Southern Hills Country Club, Tulsa, Oklahoma

This hole is 614 yards. The person I played my practice round with said you don't need a road map for this one, you need a passport.

Jay Cronley, on the fifth hole
Golf Digest, 1977

Speidel Golf Club, Wheeling, West Virginia

When you get to your ball, you're too tired to hit it.

Robyn Dummett, touring professional, c. 1970s

Spyglass Hill Golf Club, Pebble Beach, California

Pebble Beach and Cypress Point make you want to play, they're such interesting and enjoyable layouts. Spyglass Hill— that's different; that makes you want to go fishing.

Jack Nicklaus
The Greatest Game of All, 1969

Not long ago two doctors started out with three dozen golf balls. They had to send the caddie in for a new supply after six holes.

Cal Brown
Golf Digest, 1971

It's a 300-acre unplayable lie.

Jim Murray
Los Angeles Times, 1973

They ought to hang the man who designed this course. Ray Charles could have done better.

Lee Trevino
San Francisco Chronicle, 1985

Torrey Pines Golf Club, La Jolla, California

I always play better on the North Course. It's cooler over there, closer to the North Pole.

Gary McCord
San Jose Mercury News, 1984

Tournament Players Club at Eagle Trace, Coral Springs, Florida

I like the balance of the course—I shot 41–41.

Jack Nicklaus
Golf Digest, 1984

Tournament Players Club at Sawgrass, Ponte Vedra Beach, Florida

It's too early to rate this course. It's like trying to rate girls when they're born. They get better later.

Jerry Pate
San Jose Mercury News, 1982

If you birdie the eighteenth, do you win a free game?

John Mahaffey
San Francisco Examiner, 1982

It's *Star Wars* golf. The place was designed by Darth Vader.

Ben Crenshaw
Sports Illustrated, 1982

This course is ninety percent horse manure and ten percent luck.

J.C. Snead
Sports Illustrated, 1982

I've never been very good at stopping a five-iron on the hood of a car.

Jack Nicklaus
Sports Illustrated, 1982

To play well on this course you have to be both skillful and lucky, and if you are both skillful and lucky your name is Jack Nicklaus.

Chi Chi Rodriguez
Golf Digest, 1983

The only way to improve it would be to put the green on a barge and have it float around the lagoon.

Dale Hayes, on the island-green seventeenth hole
Golf Digest, 1984

It's the easiest par-five on the course.

John Mahaffey, on the par-three seventeenth
Golf Digest, 1984

Winged Foot Golf Club, Mamaroneck, New York

To match par on this course you've got to be luckier than a dog with two tails.

Sam Snead

The greens are harder than a whore's heart.

Sam Snead

A motorist attempting to leave the Winged Foot Golf Club takes a wrong turn and accidentally drives across the first green. He does no damage at all. The green holds up like asphalt.

Dick Schaap
Massacre at Winged Foot, 1974

The slope of the green has been lessened, but it is still more difficult to read than a Joycean novel.

Dick Schaap, on the tenth hole
Massacre at Winged Foot, 1974

Putting on these greens is like playing miniature golf without the boards.

Hale Irwin, at the U.S. Open, 1974

Spectator: C'mon, Johnny, hit it close.
Miller: On this course, it doesn't do any good to get it close.

Johnny Miller, at the U.S. Open, 1974

Winged Foot has the toughest eighteen finishing holes in golf.

Dave Marr
"U.S. Open," ESPN-TV, 1984

8. Diet, Exercise and Injuries

If your adversary is a hole or two down, there is no serious cause for alarm in his complaining of a severely sprained wrist. . . . Should he happen to win the next hole, these symptoms will in all probability become less troublesome.

Horace G. Hutchinson
Hints on the Game of Golf, 1886

Ben, you old sonofabitch. Just because I beat you in a playoff, you didn't have to get so mad that you tried to run a bus off the road.

Jimmy Demaret, to Hogan after his highway accident, 1949

I'm going to handle it just like a round of golf. I'm going to play it one shot at a time.

Ben Hogan, recovering from injuries, 1949

His legs weren't strong enough to carry his heart around.

Grantland Rice, on Hogan's comeback at the Los Angeles Open, 1950

I understand you have a weight problem. As you know, I have kept my weight exactly the same for years. I will be glad to send you my diet.

Jackie Gleason, telegram to Arnold Palmer, 1960s

To really lose weight playing golf, the best place to play is in Mexico. Go to any Mexican golf course, stop at every hole and drink water. Within a week you'll have reached your desired weight.

Buddy Hackett
The Truth About Golf and Other Lies, 1968

We had so little to eat that when Mom would throw a bone to the dog, he'd have to call for a fair catch.
Lee Trevino

If you're hungry, you're more alert. You're like a hungry lion. All your senses are sharpened for the kill.
Billy Casper, on why he began skipping breakfast, 1970

Five bogeys will give a guy a stomach ache every time.
Miller Barber, on why Casper skips breakfast, 1970

When I popped a couple of Rolaids.
George Archer, when asked the turning point of the match

Q: How's the food here, Roberto?
A: Like Jack Nicklaus. Very good, and very slow.
Roberto de Vicenzo, at a restaurant

Doc, your reputation is on the line. Blow this one and you can use those scalpels to eat your dinner.
Lee Trevino, before back surgery, 1976

I missed a bunch of tournaments; but considering all the hospitalization insurance I carry, I figure I wound up leading money winner.
Lee Trevino, on his surgery
Golf Digest, 1977

Somebody asked me if I run, and I said, "Not unless somebody's after me."
Sam Snead
Golf Digest, 1977

Give me a banana. I'm playing like a monkey. I might as well eat like one.

Chi Chi Rodriguez
Golf Digest, 1977

I take a lot of B's and C's. . . . And I take bone meal. That's for when I play like a dog.

Mary Dwyer, on her vitamin intake
Golf Digest, 1981

I'd probably be the fat lady in a circus right now if it hadn't been for golf. It kept me on the course and out of the refrigerator.

Kathy Whitworth
Golf Digest, 1982

With glasses I can see ants on the ground, but for some reason the ball looks too big to go in the hole.

Dick Mayer
Sports Illustrated, 1982

There was a thunderous crack like cannonfire and suddenly I was lifted a foot and a half off the ground. . . . Damn, I thought to myself, this is a helluva penalty for slow play.

Lee Trevino, on his lightning incident in 1975
They Call Me Super Mex, 1982

They say your whole life passes before you at that moment and, believe me, it does. Hey, I never knew I was so bad! I saw a lot of old girl friends.

Lee Trevino
They Call Me Super Mex, 1982

For the first time in your life, don't be afraid of a bunker.

Lee Trevino, on how to avoid lightning
"The Tonight Show," NBC-TV, 1982

We don't want to get anybody killed. Of course, if we could pick which ones, it might be a different story.
Hord Hardin, Augusta National chairman, postponing play in The Masters because of lightning, 1983

I didn't like being fat, and that's exactly what I was—fat! I used to say it was because I was big-boned, but I knew better.
Nancy Lopez
Golf Magazine, 1983

No. The golf course got in the way.
Calvin Peete, when asked if an injury had contributed to his third-round eighty-six in The Masters, 1983

I've injured both my hands playing golf and they're O.K. now, but my brain has always been somewhat suspect.
Bob Murphy
San Jose Mercury News, 1984

I'm on a grapefruit diet. I eat everything but grapefruit.
Chi Chi Rodriguez, at the Everett Open, 1984

I like to smoke and drink and I'm lazy. It's past time for me to train. I enjoy doing absolutely nothing and I'm pretty darn good at it.
Don January
Golf World, 1984

I play good when I'm home. On the road, you go to Jack in the Box, get the food and eat it in your car. Now I'm home. I can get my food at Jack in the Box and take it home. It's a lot better.
Gary McCord
San Jose Mercury News, 1984

9. Equipment

It's good sportsmanship to not pick up lost golf balls while they are still rolling.

Mark Twain

Do not be tempted to invest in a sample of each golfing invention as soon as it makes its appearance. If you do, you will only complicate and spoil your game—and encumber your locker with much useless rubbish.

Harry Vardon

Honey, why don't you quit kidding yourself? It just can't be entirely the clubs. Your trouble is *you*!

Louise Nelson, advising husband Byron, 1936

Laddie, throw me that ball. I thought so. The bugger isn't round.

Arthur Lees, British pro, after missing a thirty-foot putt, c. 1940s

The trouble that most of us find with the modern matched sets of clubs is that they don't really seem to know any more about the game than the old ones did!

Robert Browning
A History of Golf, 1955

"How are you getting on with your new clubs?" asked the golfer when he walked into the bar and saw a friend of his. "Fine," replied the friend. "They put twenty yards on my slice."

Dai Rees
Dai Rees on Golf, 1959

Talk to the ball. "This isn't going to hurt a bit," I tell the ball under my breath. "Sambo is just going to give you a nice little ride."

Sam Snead
The Education of a Golfer, 1962

George, you look perfect, . . . that beautiful knitted shirt, an alpaca sweater, those expensive slacks. . . . You've got an alligator bag, the finest matched irons, and the best woods money can buy. It's a damned shame you have to spoil it all by playing golf.

Lloyd Mangrum, to comedian George Burns

A professional will tell you the amount of flex you need in the shaft of your club. The more the flex, the more strength you will need to break the thing over your knees.

Stephen Baker
How to Play Golf in the Low 120's, 1962

Once when I was golfing in Georgia I hooked the ball into the swamp. I went in after it and found an alligator wearing a shirt with a picture of a little golfer on it.

Buddy Hackett
The Truth About Golf and Other Lies, 1968

I've been a test pilot for Foot Joy forever. I test their sixty-five-dollar alligator models to see if standing in them for long periods of time in a bar brings them any serious harm. What effect spilling beer has on them.

George Low, former touring professional, 1970

You know the old rule. He who have fastest cart never have to play bad lie.

Mickey Mantle
Esquire, 1971

I'd give up golf if I didn't have so many sweaters.

Bob Hope, 1972

Never wear hand-me-downs, freebies, borrowed togs or Christmas presents.

Doug Sanders, on how to become a better dresser
Come Swing With Me, 1974

Bing Crosby, who once lived on the "slice" side of the fourteenth fairway at Pebble Beach, was reported never to have had to buy a ball in his life.

Henry Longhurst
The Best of Henry Longhurst, 1978

I was gonna buy me one of them Johnny Miller leisure suits . . . but the dude said the fire marshall took 'em off the racks! They don't make no medium dumpy anyway.

Lee Trevino
Golf Digest, 1978

Where'd you get this ugly thing? Man, this is one of them airport drivers. That's right! You hit this thing for two days, miss the cut and go to the airport!

Lee Trevino
Golf Digest, 1978

I don't like Number Four balls. And I don't like fives, sixes, or sevens on my cards.

George Archer, on his superstitions, 1979

Willis' Rule of Golf: You can't lose an old golf ball.

John Willis, television sportscaster, 1980

I wear black. I loved Westerns and the cowboys always looked good in black.

Gary Player

Baffling late-life discovery. Golfers wear those awful clothes on *purpose.*

Herb Caen
San Francisco Chronicle, 1980

I'm a traditionalist. I want to play a white ball. But a manufacturer wouldn't have to offer me a million dollars to change my mind.

Chi Chi Rodriguez
Golf Magazine, 1982

I have seen mink headcovers, bamboo shafts, concave sand wedges, the twelve-wood, the seven-and-a-half iron, floating balls, linoleum shoes, dome-shaped tees, distance measurers, girdles that keep your elbows together, . . . and putters as ugly as Stillson wrenches. But the silliest thing I have ever seen in golf is the headcover that goes with the ball retriever.

Charles Price
Golfer-At-Large, 1982

There is one more important characteristic: it must have a large and smooth area for advertising material. That, above all, is the purpose of golf hats.

Peter Dobereiner
Golf Digest, 1982

Never, never, never, never, will I ever be able to force myself to hit a pink golf ball. After all, the line has to be drawn somewhere.

Peter Dobereiner
Golf Digest, 1983

I used to use three a round, but since I bought the company I only use one.

Jack Nicklaus, on MacGregor golf gloves
Golf Digest, 1983

My tournament lineup would include . . . any guy who just bought a new club called a Birdie-Seeker or FlagJammer or a putter that looks like something you'd fix the plumbing with.

Jim Murray
Los Angeles Times, 1983

How about knickers? Can you imagine anything sillier than a man wearing knickers? That's like putting Bermuda shorts on an alligator.

Charles Price
Golf Digest, 1983

I feel like Spiderman.

Fuzzy Zoeller, on his rubber-spiked golf shoes
Golf Digest, 1984

Those clubs have no idea how old Lee is.

Jackie Burke, on Trevino's new clubs and improved play
USA Today, 1984

Did you know that a seven-iron thrown into a water hazard begins to rust after only forty-eight hours? Do you call that workmanship?

Peter Andrews
Golf Digest, 1984

10. Famous Last Words

It's a shame, but he'll never make a golfer—too much temper.
Alex Smith, Scottish professional, on Bobby Jones, 1915

You'll never get anywhere fooling around those golf courses.
Clara Hogan, to son Ben at age sixteen, 1929

Mister Gene, you got to hit the three-wood if you want to clear that water.
Stovepipe, caddie of Gene Sarazen, before his 220-yard four-wood for a double eagle at The Masters, 1935

Hey, hurry up, Gene, I got a date tonight.
Walter Hagen, to Sarazen before his famous shot, 1935

If I didn't have to throw that tomato for a living, I'd take this game up in a serious way and win all the championships. And this is one course I'd tear wide open.
Dizzy Dean, St. Louis Cardinals pitcher, on Oakmont, site of the U.S. Open, 1935

Would you like to know how to sink those putts? Just hit the ball a little closer to the hole.
Valerie Hogan, to husband Ben during the Los Angeles Open, 1937

Pick the ball up, have the clubs destroyed, and leave the course.

> **Viscount Castlerosse, British columnist, to his caddie after topping three straight shots, c. 1930s**

If I'da cleared the trees and drove the green, it woulda been a great tee shot.

> **Sam Snead, 1954**

His type come and go every year.

> **Charles Price, quoting his editors at the *Saturday Evening Post* who refused a feature story on Arnold Palmer, 1955**

Yes, a lot more people beat me now.

> **Dwight D. Eisenhower, asked if his game had changed since leaving the White House**

I can beat the fat kid the best day he ever had.

> **Arnold Palmer, after losing the U.S. Open playoff to Jack Nicklaus, 1962**

No matter how hard I try, I just *can't* seem to break sixty-four.

> **Jack Nicklaus**

I'm not afraid of Jack. If you play better than he does, you can beat him.

> **Tom Weiskopf**

He was standing too close to my ball.

> **Barry M. Goldwater, after beaning a spectator thirty yards off the tee at the Phoenix Open pro-am, 1965**

Do Janie a favor. Tell her to get off the tour. Nobody who swings like Shirley Temple can make a living in this game.

Richie Ferraris, father of Jan Ferraris, on Jane Blalock, 1969

I can't win anything but money.

Frank Beard, leading the tour in money-winnings without having won a tournament, 1969

I figure on going for another six years until I'm forty. Then I'll try the pro golf circuit. I'm as good right now as any of them.

Evel Knievel, stunt man
Sports Illustrated, 1972

Well, I guess all those years of practice finally paid off.

Jack Nicklaus II, age nine, after breaking fifty for nine holes, 1973

You want to be out there because you are a good golfer, not because you are wearing something. I don't think a good player has to dress differently or stop wearing makeup to win tournaments.

Laura Cole, winless in eleven years on the LPGA Tour
Golf Magazine, 1981

He looks like a pretty good player indeed. But what do I know? I'm the guy who said Lee Trevino would never make it out here!

Raymond Floyd, on Tim Norris
Golf Magazine, 1982

Those guys don't intimidate me. I can beat them.

Jodie Mudd, within two strokes of the lead at The Masters, shot a final-round eighty-six, 1983

During the seventies, I wasn't a good striker of the ball at all.
Oh, I won a lot of tournaments.

> **Jack Nicklaus, who won eight majors in the '70s**
> *The New Yorker,* 1983

Now that I'm a high school graduate, all kinds of opportunities should open up for me next year.

> **Calvin Peete, a millionaire on the tour, on passing his**
> **high school equivalency test**
> *Sports Illustrated,* 1982

I always thought the game was silly. Who wants to chase a
little ball around under the hot sun?

> **Calvin Peete, on why he didn't take up golf**
> **at an early age**
> *San Francisco Chronicle,* 1983

I was stubborn. I knew the four-iron was the right club.

> **Ben Crenshaw, on knocking three balls in the water**
> **for an eleven at the fourteenth hole, Sea Pines**
> **Heritage Classic, 1983**

I shoot at the stick.

> **Mancil Davis, on how he has scored forty-two aces**
> *Golf Magazine,* 1983

I was worried about the people behind me getting mad because we would play so slow.

> **Karen DiSabella, a twenty-three-year-old secretary**
> **from Stonington, Connecticut, who aced the first**
> **hole she ever played, 1984**

I know I'm getting better at golf because I'm hitting fewer
spectators.

> **Gerald R. Ford, 1984**

11. Fans

My gallery at the end consisted of my two opponents, three caddies, and some guy who was in the Army with me and wanted to borrow ten bucks.

Cary Middlecoff, en route to a seventy-eight, 1949

In a stroke-play tournament, with so much going on all over the course simultaneously, more often than not an observer finds himself stationed intently just where nothing is happening.

Herbert Warren Wind
"Nine Strokes in 27 Holes," 1961

I'm a hot-dog pro. That's when someone in the gallery looks at his pairing sheet and says, "Here comes Joe Baloney, Sam Sausage, and Chi Chi Rodriguez. Let's go get a hot dog."

Chi Chi Rodriguez, at the PGA, 1964

It is a gallery that revels in disaster. "Palmer just took an eight!" will ring through it from time to time, and the town criers who hurry from fairway to fairway with the bad news are as happy as an old maid reporting a new divorce.

Jim Murray, on the Los Angeles Open
The Sporting World of Jim Murray, 1968

If the crowd won't applaud for me, I'll do it myself.

Leonard Thompson, after hitting a good sand wedge, 1974

If I had been in the gallery, I'd have gone home.
**Johnny Miller, after a thirty-nine on the front side
at the Bing Crosby National Pro-Am, 1975**

Rule One: Whenever a spectator seeks out a really good vantage point and settles down on shooting stick or canvas chair, the tallest and fattest golf watcher on the course will take up station directly in front.

Peter Dobereiner
Golf World, 1975

The crowds are so large, especially around the name players, that one can travel eighteen holes and never see a shot. But it's the finest tournament you'll ever hear.

Mark Mulvoy and Art Spander, on The Masters
Golf: The Passion and the Challenge, 1977

A Fort Worth doctor caught in the act of leering at a nifty in a thin halter told me: "It's O.K. I have a clearance from my wife to leer at anything above a 36-B cup."

**Gary Cartwright, on the Colonial National
Invitation tournament**
Texas Monthly, 1977

The hero-worshippers in his gallery ought to appreciate that somebody has to play along with Arnold to keep his score if nothing else.

Dave Hill
Teed Off, 1977

I drew a big gallery today. I was paired with Palmer.

Gene Littler

I don't like to watch golf on television. I can't stand whispering.

David Brenner, comic, 1978

Heck, I wish they'd make the gallery ropes out of bounds. We're the only sport that plays in the audience.

Lee Trevino
Sports Illustrated, 1979

Watching golf on TV is one thing. Trying to watch a golf tournament in person is like trying to cover a war on foot.

Jay Cronley
Playboy, 1981

I told 'em, "If you want to laugh, you have two choices: Either go to a circus or I'll bury this eight-iron in your head."

David Graham, to fans at the British Open, 1981

A woman had me autograph a five-dollar bill once and told me she would keep it for the rest of her life. A half-hour later, I bought some drinks with a twenty. The change came back, and the five was in it.

Lee Trevino
Detroit Free Press, 1982

I can't figure out where they all came from—even Thursday and Friday. I thought people worked during the week.

Carol Rissel, Bing Crosby National Pro-Am executive committee
San Francisco Examiner, 1982

A number of years ago, it dawned on me that the biggest seller at golf tournaments were those periscopes.

Deane Beman, PGA Tour Commissioner, on the origin of stadium golf
Golf Digest, 1983

Golf fans have a remarkable sixth sense that tells them what is happening elsewhere on the course, often a mile away. Some sort of telepathic wizardry takes place that not even the Soviet Union's KGB could figure out.

Dan Hruby
San Jose Mercury News, 1983

12. Foreign Venues

Golf is a typical capitalist lunacy of upper-class Edwardian England.

George Bernard Shaw

Individually, they are pretty nice folks. But get them together and they are about as miserable a bunch of people as you could ever have the misfortune to run into in a supposedly civilized world.

Tommy Bolt, on the British
Los Angeles Times, 1957

"Are those mosquitoes dangerous?" I asked the hotel manager. "Not if you've had spotted fever, malaria, and dengue fever," he said.

Sam Snead, in the Belgian Congo
The Education of a Golfer, 1962

I only came here because I heard the Irish hate the British as much as I do.

Dave Hill, playing in Dublin

Everyone is studying golf technique like mad. Every young lad now aspires to be another Palmer or another Nicklaus. We may go centuries before we produce another playwright.

Joe Carr, Irish amateur
The New Yorker, 1967

It has been estimated that more golf poetry exists in Scotland than heather.

Dan Jenkins
The Dogged Victims of Inexorable Fate, 1970

What else is there to do over there? Wear a skirt?

George Low, on golf in Scotland

We had to eat everything with our fingers, except a piece of fish. They gave me a toothpick to eat that. Hell, I've got a cat back home in Texas who eats with a fork!

Lee Trevino, at the British Open, Muirfield, Scotland, 1972

A stroke may be played again if interrupted by gunfire or sudden explosion.

Local club rule, Rhodesia, 1972

After all these years, it's still embarrassing for me to play on the American golf tour. Like the time I asked my caddie for a sand wedge and he came back ten minutes later with a ham on rye.

Chi Chi Rodriguez, Puerto Rican touring pro

Certainly they [the greens] are the greenest, which is hardly surprising in a country where housewives habitually peep out of their cottage windows and observe that it is a beautiful day for hanging the washing out to rinse.

Peter Dobereiner, on Ireland
The Glorious World of Golf, 1973

I had this prejudice against the British, until I discovered that fifty percent of them were female.

Raymond Floyd
Golf Digest, 1977

All I could think of was those movies and what Texans did to strangers they didn't like. Nine out of ten they get lynched. I really was afraid I might get lynched.

Bruce Crampton, Australian professional, playing in the Houston Open in 1957
Golf Digest, 1978

I love it here in the United States. In Japan I have no privacy. In the States I can have a hole in my jeans and nobody will notice.

Ayako Okamoto
The Sporting News, 1984

Every round I play I shorten my life by two years.

Tommy Nakajima, Japanese professional, on the tough tour courses in the United States, 1984

In Britain, you skip the ball, hop it, bump it, run it, hit under it, on top of it and then hope for the right bounce.

Doug Sanders
Sports Illustrated, 1984

I have to save it. It's our national bird.

Chi Chi Rodriguez, Puerto Rican professional, as a bug crawled across Dave Stockton's putting path, 1984

Birkdale Golf Club, Royal, Southport,
Lancashire, England

At fifteen, we put down my bag to hunt for a ball—found the
ball, lost the bag.

Lee Trevino
Sports Illustrated, 1983

Carnoustie Golf Club, Carnoustie, Scotland

I've got a lawn mower back in Texas, I'll send it over.

Ben Hogan, at the British Open, 1953

A good swamp, spoiled.

Gary Player
Golf World, 1975

Tom Watson likens Carnoustie to an ugly old woman who at
least is honest with you: when you add up your score after
your round, she tells you what she thinks of you.

Herbert Warren Wind
The New Yorker, 1981

Dornoch Golf Club, Royal, Dornoch,
Sutherland, Scotland

When you play it, you get the feeling you could be living
just as easily in the eighteen-hundreds, or even the seventeen-
hundreds. If an old Scot in a red jacket had popped out from
behind a sand dune, beating a feather ball, I wouldn't have
blinked an eye.

Peter Dye, golf course architect
The New Yorker, 1964

Muirfield, Muirfield, East Lothian, Scotland

You take a search warrant to get in, and a wedge and a prayer to get out.

Harold Henning, South African pro, on the seaside rough

Prestwick Golf Club, Prestwick, Ayrshire, Scotland

The green was there, all right, as are all of the greens at Prestwick, but you never see them until you are on them, which is usually eight or ten strokes after leaving the tee.

Dan Jenkins
The Dogged Victims of Inexorable Fate, 1970

St. Andrews Golf Club, Royal, St. Andrews, Fife, Scotland

You can play a damned good shot there and find the ball in a damned bad place!

George Duncan, British professional
The American Golfer, 1923

Say, that looks like an old, abandoned golf course. What did they call it?

Sam Snead, upon first seeing St. Andrews, 1946

There's nothing wrong with the St. Andrews course that a hundred bulldozers couldn't put right.

Ed Furgol, American touring professional

The Old Course needs a dry clean and press.

Ed Furgol

The only place over there that's holier than St. Andrews is Westminster Abbey.

Sam Snead
The Education of a Golfer, 1962

In the galleries, there were lots of dogs, which never barked, and lots of children, who didn't howl or fuss, which is the way it is in Scotland.

Herbert Warren Wind
The New Yorker, 1970

The Road Hole, the seventeenth, is the most famous and infamous hole. . . . As a planner and builder of golf holes worldwide, I have no hesitation in allowing that if one built such a hole today you would be sued for incompetence.

Peter Thomson
Golf Digest, 1984

The reason the Road Hole is the greatest par-four in the world is because it's a par-five.

Ben Crenshaw
Sports Illustrated, 1984

13. Friendly Matches

If golfers keep on playing so slowly, on the green particularly, one way to correct the situation is to knock your ball into the SOBs. There will be a slight delay while you have a hell of a fight, but from that point on you will move faster.

Horace G. Hutchinson
Hints on the Game of Golf, 1886

Remember, they were friends. For years they had shared each other's sorrows, joys, and golf balls, and sliced into the same bunkers.

P. G. Wodehouse
"A Woman Is Only a Woman," 1919

The least thing upset him on the links. He missed short putts because of the uproar of butterflies in the adjoining meadows.

P. G .Wodehouse
"The Unexpected Clicking of Cuthbert," 1921

It is a law of nature that everybody plays a hole badly when going through.

Bernard Darwin
Playing the Like, 1934

Man, to threesome: Mind if I play through? My wife's having a pretty tricky operation and I'd like to get to the hospital as soon as I can.

David Langdon, cartoon
The New Yorker, 1952

You must expect anything in golf. A stranger comes through, he's keen for a game, he seems affable enough, and on the eighth fairway he turns out to be an idiot.

Alistair Cooke, journalist, 1957

It's a funny thing, Bob. I've just lent Bolivia millions of dollars, but I only have one buck on me to pay with.

Dwight D. Eisenhower, paying off a golfing bet with Bob Hope

I confess that I have played rounds where the other three players in the foursome became total strangers to me in the long distances between tee and green.

Milton Gross
Eighteen Holes in My Head, 1959

You don't much care in the mixed game whether you win or lose. All you want to do is make a jackass out of your male opponent and get his partner to flare up at him, which can sometimes be amusing.

> **Rex Lardner**
> *Out of the Bunker and Into the Trees,* 1960

Many a golf course and many a big gambler would have eaten me up if I hadn't eaten them first by having a mean frame of mind.

> **Sam Snead**
> *The Education of a Golfer,* 1962

You can imagine my consternation when I was invited to play at this place. . . . Usually, I play golf with the kind of people who rob banks, not own them.

> **Jim Murray, on playing at the Los**
> **Angeles Country Club**
> *The Sporting World of Jim Murray,* 1968

I used to play to a six handicap and now I play to a twelve. Not only that, it now takes me five and a half hours to complete a round.

> **Don Walker, Florida neighbor of Jack Nicklaus**
> **and Dr. Cary Middlecoff**

I play with friends, but we don't play friendly games.

> **Ben Hogan**
> *Golf Digest,* 1970

Gimme: An agreement between two losers who can't putt.

> **Jim Bishop, syndicated column, 1970**

There's no better game in the world when you are in good
company, and no worse game when you are in bad company.
Tommy Bolt
The Hole Truth, 1971

Give me a millionaire with a bad backswing and I can have
a very pleasant afternoon.
George Low

I never lied about my handicap; I just let my opponents talk
themselves into a trap.
Bobby Riggs
Court Hustler, 1973

The only difference I was aware of between Democrats and
Republicans was that Republicans seemed to have lower
handicaps and more sets of clubs while Democrats like to bet
more—and paid off quicker.
Dan Jenkins
Dead Solid Perfect, 1974

Somebody asked me one time why I didn't turn pro. Man, I
can't afford it.
Dick Martin, Texas golf hustler

Never bet with anyone you meet on the first tee who has a
deep suntan, a one-iron in his bag and squinty eyes.
Dave Marr

It's amazing how many people in the world almost walk
around looking to be hustled.
Dave Hill
Teed Off, 1977

Some guys get so nervous playing for their own money, the greens don't need fertilizing for a year.

Dave Hill
Teed Off, 1977

I've just heard that soon he might be well enough to play golf. Hasn't the man suffered enough?

Paul Harvey, radio commentator, on artificial-heart-transplant patient Barney Clark
Golf Digest, 1983

Seve, I wouldn't give my mother two strokes a side.

Tommy Bolt, to Seve Ballesteros, on a television ad for golf clubs, 1984

They play for big bucks at private clubs, too, but there's a difference. They can afford to lose.

Hale Irwin
Golf Digest, 1984

My car absolutely will not run unless my golf clubs are in the trunk.

Bruce Berlet, golf writer, *Hartford Courant*, 1984

You don't necessarily have to bring your clubs to play golf—just lie about your score.

Lon Simmons, Oakland A's broadcaster

There's an old saying: If a man comes home with sand in his cuffs and cockleburs in his pants, don't ask him what he shot.

Sam Snead
USA Today, 1984

My worst day on the golf course still beats my best day in the office.

John Hallisey, Monterey *Peninsula-Herald* golf writer, 1984

14. Golf: General Thoughts

I do not remember having met any golfer who did not consider himself on the whole a remarkably unlucky one.

Horace G. Hutchinson
Hints on the Game of Golf, 1886

Excessive golfing dwarfs the intellect. And is this to be wondered at when we consider that the more fatuously vacant the mind is, the better for play.

Sir Walter Simpson
The Art of Golf, 1887

Golf is a good walk spoiled.

Mark Twain

The wit of man has never invented a pastime equal to golf for its healthful recreation, its pleasurable excitement, and its never ending source of amusement.

Lord Balfour, British statesman

Golf is an indispensable adjunct to high civilization.

Andrew Carnegie, American industrialist, on leaving $200,000 to Yale to build a golf course

Golf is so popular simply because it is the best game in the world at which to be bad. . . . At golf it is the bad player who gets the most strokes.

A. A. Milne
Not That It Matters, 1919

Golf is twenty percent mechanics and technique. The other eighty percent is philosophy, humor, tragedy, romance, melodrama, companionship, camaraderie, cussedness, and conversation.

Grantland Rice, sportswriter, 1920

It was a morning when all nature shouted "Fore!" The breeze, as it blew gently up from the valley, seemed to bring a message of hope and cheer, whispering of chip-shots holed and brassies landing squarely on the meat.

P. G. Wodehouse
"The Heart of a Goof," 1923

I guess there is nothing that will get your mind off everything like golf will. I have never been depressed enough to take up the game, but they say you can get so sore at yourself that you forget to hate your enemies.

Will Rogers

Golf is like a love affair: if you don't take it seriously, it's not fun; if you do take it seriously, it breaks your heart.

Arnold Daly
Reader's Digest, 1933

Golf may be . . . a sophisticated game. At least, it is usually played with the outward appearance of great dignity. It is, nevertheless, a game of considerable passion, either of the explosive type, or that which burns inwardly and sears the soul.

Bobby Jones

The terrible thing about a missed shot in golf is that the thing is done, irrevocably, irretrievably. Perhaps that is why golf is so great a game; it is so much like the game of life. We don't have the shots over in either.

O. B. Keeler, Atlanta sportswriter

Golf is the Esperanto of sport. All over the world golfers talk the same language—much of it nonsense and much unprintable—endure the same frustrations, discover the same infallible secrets of putting, share the same illusory joys.

Henry Longhurst
Round in Sixty-Eight, 1953

Like life, golf can be humbling. However, little good comes from brooding about mistakes we've made. The next shot, in golf or in life, is the big one.

Grantland Rice
The Tumult and the Shouting, 1954

It is this constant and undying hope for improvement that makes golf so exquisitely worth the playing.

Bernard Darwin, British golf writer

I've been around golf courses all my life. They are the Demaret answer to the world's problems. When I get out on that green carpet called a fairway and manage to poke the ball right down the middle, my surroundings look like a touch of heaven on earth.

Jimmy Demaret
My Partner, Ben Hogan, 1954

If you watch a game, it's fun. If you play it, it's recreation. If you work at it, it's golf.

Bob Hope
Reader's Digest, 1958

Golf does strange things to other people, too. It makes liars out of honest men, cheats out of altruists, cowards out of brave men and fools out of everybody.

Milton Gross
Eighteen Holes in My Head, 1959

One reward golf has given me, and I shall always be thankful for it, is introducing me to some of the world's most picturesque, tireless and bald-faced liars.

Rex Lardner
Out of the Bunker and Into the Trees, 1960

Golf is essentially an exercise in masochism conducted out-of-doors; it affords opportunity for a certain swank, it induces a sense of kinship in its victims, and it forces them to breathe fresh air, but it is, at bottom, an elaborate and addictive rite calculated to drive them crazy for hours on end and send them straight to the whisky bottle after that.

Paul O'Neil
Life, 1962

If you don't succeed at first, don't despair. Remember, it takes time to learn to play golf; most players spend their entire lifetime finding out about the game before they give it up.

Stephen Baker
How to Play Golf in the Low 120's, 1962

Gentlemen play golf. And if you aren't a gentleman when you start, after the crushing events of the game, you surely become one.

Bing Crosby

Golf is more fun than walking naked in a strange place, but not much.

Buddy Hackett
The Truth About Golf and Other Lies, 1968

It was named by drunken Scots after listening to barking dogs. Golf is played by twenty million mature American men whose wives think they are out there having fun.

Jim Bishop, syndicated column, 1970

It is sometimes said that only when he stands at the altar on his wedding day does a man experience quite the same sensation of impending doom as he feels each week on the first tee of a Sunday morning.

Norman Mair
"Of Games and Golf"

That was the trouble with golf, I thought. Only a golfer could ever understand why anyone would play the stupid, f____ game.

Dan Jenkins
Dead Solid Perfect, 1974

Golf is neither a microcosm of nor a metaphor for Life. It is a sport, a bloodless sport, if you don't count ulcers.

Dick Schaap
Massacre at Winged Foot, 1974

There are now more golf clubs in the world than Gideon Bibles, more golf balls than missionaries and, if every golfer in the world, male and female, were laid end to end, I for one would leave them there.

Michael Parkinson, president, Anti-Golf Society
Sunday Times (London), 1975

Golf is an open exhibition of overweening ambition, courage deflated by stupidity, skill soured by a whiff of arrogance. . . . These humiliations are the essence of the game.

Alistair Cooke, journalist

Golf is the only sport where a man [of] sixty can play with the best. That's why golf is such a great game. And no one has ever licked it.

Sam Snead
Golf Digest, 1975

The game was easy for me as a kid, and I had to play a while to find out how hard it is.

Raymond Floyd, after winning The Masters, 1976

Golf is like art; it's impossible to be perfect.

Sandra Palmer
Golf Magazine, 1977

Indeed, the highest pleasure of golf may be that on the fairways and far from all the pressures of commerce and rationality, we can feel immortal for a few hours.

Colman McCarthy
The Pleasures of the Game, 1977

Good golf isn't a matter of hitting great shots. It's finding a way to make your bad ones not so bad. If I hadn't learned to do that, you'd still be thinking "Trevino" is Italian.

Lee Trevino
Golf Digest, 1979

A hundred years of experience has demonstrated that the game is temporary insanity practiced in a pasture.

Dave Kindred
Washington Post, 1979

To see one's ball gallop two hundred and more yards down the fairway, or to see it fly from the face of an eight-iron clear across an entire copse of maples in full autumnal flare, is to join one's soul with the vastness that, contemplated from another angle, intimidates the spirit, and makes one feel small.

John Updike
"Updike's Adventures in Golf's Wonderland," 1982

The golfer has more enemies than any other athlete. He has 14 clubs in his bag, all of them different; 18 holes to play, all of *them* different, every week; and all around him are sand, trees, grass, water, wind and 143 other players. In addition, the game is fifty percent mental, so his biggest enemy is himself.

Dan Jenkins
Sports Illustrated, 1982

Good night, this game teaches you a lot about yourself. You can tell by the way a guy walks how he's doing.

Ben Crenshaw
Golf Digest, 1983

Golf combines two favorite American pastimes: taking long walks and hitting things with a stick.

P. J. O'Rourke
Modern Manners, 1983

Golf is like fishing and hunting. What counts is the companionship and fellowship of friends, not what you catch or shoot.

George Archer
Golf Digest, 1984

Good companionship? Have you ever actually listened to golfers talking to each other? "Looked good starting out." "Better direction than last time." "Who's away?" It sounds like a visitors' day at a home for the criminally insane.

Peter Andrews
Golf Digest, 1984

Golf is the cruelest of sports. Like life, it's unfair. It's a harlot. A trollop. It leads you on. It never lives up to its promises. It's not a sport, it's bondage. An obsession. A boulevard of broken dreams. It plays with men. And runs off with the butcher.

Jim Murray
Los Angeles Times, 1985

15. Golf and Other Sports

It's just the old-fashioned pool hall moved outdoors, but with no chairs around the walls.

Will Rogers, on golf

Golf tournaments are lonely. In baseball there's eight other guys to keep me company.

Walter Hagen, when asked why he wanted to play baseball instead of golf, 1913

When I hit a ball, I want someone else to go chase it.

Rogers Hornsby, baseball player

In other games you get another chance. In baseball you get three cracks at it; in tennis you lose only one point. But in golf the loss of one shot has been responsible for the loss of heart.

Tommy Armour

Yeh, no more golf for me. But I tell you, Buchanan, maybe if you aren't busy tomorrow we could meet on the first tee at nine tomorrow morning, because if I'm going to quit I might as well get in one more game.

Babe Ruth, to Florida pro J. A. Buchanan

I think golf is good for boxing, but the reverse is far from being the case.

Max Baer, former heavyweight champion, 1937

In tennis you seldom have a chance, once things get going, to get shaky. You're too busy running around like a race horse. But in golf—hell, it makes me nervous just to talk about it. That little white ball just sits there. A man can beat himself before he ever swings at it.

Ellsworth Vines, tennis champion who later became a professional golfer

In golf, when we hit a foul ball, we got to go out and play it.

Sam Snead, to Ted Williams

I just shook a hand that felt like five bands of steel.

Ted Williams, upon meeting Ben Hogan, 1951

The pay is great, and the only way you can get hurt playing golf is by getting struck by lightning.

Ted Williams, on professional golf

Golf is cow-pasture pool.

O. K. Brovard, St. Louis *Post-Dispatch* editor

One of the advantages bowling has over golf is that you seldom lose a bowling ball.

Don Carter, professional bowler

The only reason I ever played golf in the first place was so I could afford to hunt and fish.

Sam Snead, hinting about retirement
***Sports Illustrated*, 1968**

Whitey Ford . . . golfs like he pitches. He puts the ball where he wants it—low and away.

> **Jim Murray**
> *The Sporting World of Jim Murray*, 1968

One point on which all golfers can immediately agree is that, whatever else golf may be, it is not a game. How much simpler life would be if it were just a game, like tennis.

> **Peter Dobereiner**
> *The Glorious World of Golf*, 1973

In baseball you hit a home run over the right-field fence, the left-field fence, the center-field fence. In golf everything has got to be right over second base.

> **Ken Harrelson, former baseball player who took up professional golf**

Brodie: Anybody see it?
Spectator: Yeah, it was intercepted.

> **John Brodie, San Francisco 49ers quarterback, at the Bing Crosby National Pro-Am**

My best score ever is 103. But I've only been playing fifteen years.

> **Alex Karras, former NFL defensive lineman**

Thanks a lot for curing my slice. Now what can you do for my hook?

> **Jim Palmer, baseball pitcher, to pro Dave Stockton**
> *Golf Digest*, 1977

Thanks, Bill, but you really shouldn't have done that. When I coached football and got down to the one-foot line, nobody ever said it was good.

> **Jess Neely, former football coach, to a friend who conceded a putt**
> *Golf Digest*, 1977

It took me seventeen years to get three thousand hits in base-ball. I did it in one afternoon on the golf course.

Hank Aaron

I'd do better if the ball were two feet off the ground and moving.

Stan Musial
Golf Digest, 1978

No, I didn't play football. I wasn't good enough. Never considered it, really. I always felt that I'd like to keep all of my blood inside my body.

Howard Twitty, 6'5", 220 pounds
Golf Digest, 1978

I played mixed doubles with a whole new foursome yesterday and I explained that golf was really my game. Of course, I told my golfing foursome today that tennis was really my game.

Dinah Shore
Golf Magazine, 1981

Too bad there aren't water hazards in baseball like there are in golf. We could lose all the balls and go home.

Lon Simmons, Oakland A's announcer,
during a dull game, 1981

Hitting a golf ball correctly is the most sophisticated and complicated maneuver in all of sport, with the possible exception of eating a hot dog at a ball game without getting mustard on your shirt.

Ray Fitzgerald
Golf Digest, 1981

It's the first time a .200 hitter ever had anything named after him.

Bob Hope, on the Joe Garagiola Tucson Open
Golf Digest, 1981

It's a lot easier hitting a quarterback than a little white ball.
**Bubba Smith, to Dick Butkus on the Miller
Lite Beer commercials, 1982**

The first time he ever let himself get talked into a celebrity golf tournament, he shot a score of 115. It was his own fault. He counted all his strokes.

Bob Uecker, on pitcher Bob Gibson
Catcher in the Wry, 1982

He could hit a ball farther off line than any man I ever knew. When Sandy practiced he would blanket three fairways, three hundred yards out and three hundred yards wide. He was like a one-man hailstorm.

**Mac Hunter, Riviera Country Club professional,
on former pitcher Sandy Koufax**
Golf Digest, 1982

What we have to do is get Dwight Clark to stand in the middle of the fairway about two hundred yards away. Joe would hit him out of habit.

**Cass Montana, on her husband, quarterback
Joe Montana**
San Jose Mercury News, 1983

Why shouldn't he [infielder Pete O'Brien] have a good attitude? He was raised in Pebble Beach. Wouldn't you have a good attitude if your biggest decision every morning was whether to play Spyglass Hill or Cypress Point?

Doug Rader, Texas Rangers manager, 1983

In football . . . some coaches have stated, "When you throw a pass, three things can happen, two of them are bad." In golf, there is no limit.

> **Marino Parascenzo**
> *Golf Magazine,* 1983

My handicap is that I don't have a big enough beer cooler for the back of my golf car.

> **Rick D'Amico, Houston Gamblers linebacker**
> *Golf Digest,* 1983

My handicap? Woods and irons.

> **Chris Codiroli, Oakland A's pitcher, 1983**

Golf is nobody's game.

> **Willie Mays, at the Bing Crosby National Pro-Am, 1983**

Everybody survives slumps, . . . except maybe boxers. If they have a bad streak, they get knocked on their cans.

> **Tom Watson**
> *Sports Illustrated,* 1984

That's the way Tom is, always analyzing everything. When we play golf together, he's always telling me exactly how I should grip the club. I tell him I don't want to hear that shit. Just let me hit the ball.

> **Jim Rice, Boston Red Sox outfielder, on pitcher Tom Seaver**
> *San Francisco Chronicle,* 1984

Big-league baseball players are the worst. . . . They swing with power, don't ask for advice, and invariably hit to all fields.

> **Tommy Bolt**

I think golf is the hardest sport to play. . . . One day you're up on Cloud Nine and the next day you couldn't scratch a whale's belly.

> **Sam Snead**
> *San Francisco Chronicle*, 1984

I'd rather play Dallas.

> **Eddie DeBartolo, Jr., San Francisco 49ers owner, on playing Pebble Beach**
> *San Jose Mercury News*, 1984

16. Golf and Politics

I find it difficult to squeeze in the claims of both golf and politics into the twenty-four hours.

> **Lord Balfour, British statesman**

I did not see the sense in chasing a little white ball around a field.

> **Calvin Coolidge, on why he never played golf**

You get to know more of the character of a man in a round of golf than you can get to know in six months with only political experience.

> **David Lloyd George, British statesman**
> *The Observer* (London), 1924

No man has mastered golf until he has realized that his good shots are accidents and his bad shots good exercise.

> **Eugene R. Black, American government official**

Rail-splitting produced an immortal President in Lincoln, but golf hasn't produced even a good A-1 Congressman.

Will Rogers, American humorist

Here you are, the greatest golfer in the world, being introduced by the worst one.

James J. Walker, Mayor of New York, at a City Hall ceremony honoring Bobby Jones, 1930

If I had my way, any man guilty of golf would be ineligible for any public office in the United States, and the families of the breed would be shipped off to the white slave corrals of the Argentine.

H. L. Mencken, American journalist

Golf is a game whose aim is to hit a very small ball into an even smaller hole, with weapons singularly ill-designed for the purpose.

Sir Winston Churchill, British statesman

Playing the game, I have learned the meaning of humility. It has given me an understanding of the futility of human effort.

Abba Eban, Israeli ambassador

Augusta is the course Ike Eisenhower usually plays on. That's proof enough for me that he is a man with good taste.

Jimmy Demaret
My Partner, Ben Hogan, 1954

President Eisenhower has given up golf for painting—it takes fewer strokes.

Bob Hope

Did you read where Arnold Palmer has been talking about the governorship of Pennsylvania? Man, I think that hip injury must be moving up to his *head.*

> Dave Marr, 1968

The last time I played a round with Vice President Agnew he hit a birdie—an eagle, a Moose, an Elk and a Mason.

> **Bob Hope**

Sanders won $200 in the tournament, and that just paid for the medical attention he required.

> **Spiro T. Agnew, after Agnew's errant shot hit Doug Sanders in the Bob Hope Desert Classic**
> *Golf Digest*, 1970

At least he can't cheat on his score—because all you have to do is look back down the fairway and count the wounded.

> **Bob Hope, on Spiro T. Agnew, 1971**

I said a few unprintable words under my breath and called it a Mulligan.

> **Alan Shepard, on his missed six-iron on the moon, 1971**

Golf acts as a corrective against sinful pride. I attribute the insane arrogance of the later Roman emperors almost entirely to the fact that, never having played golf, they never knew that strange chastening humility which is engendered by a topped chip shot.

> **P. G. Wodehouse**
> *P. G. Wodehouse on Golf*, 1973

I'm aware that golf is probably some kind of a mental disorder like gambling or women or politics.

> **Dan Jenkins**
> *Dead Solid Perfect*, 1974

Golf is a humbling game, yes, but with one solid stroke of the ball a pro can imagine himself a colossus, greater than Einstein, Rockefeller, and all the generals of the armies.

Al Barkow
Golf's Golden Grind, 1974

Actually, most of us don't follow politics closely, but if we did we'd probably be somewhere to the right of Barry Goldwater.

Dave Hill, on his fellow pros
Golf Digest, 1975

If I swung the gavel the way I swung that golf club, the nation would be in a helluva mess.

Tip O'Neill, Speaker of the House
Golf Digest, 1980

Somebody asked me the other day about this Parkinson woman some of the [House] members are supposed to be involved with. I told them that at my stage of life the greatest thrill a guy gets is sinking a forty-foot putt.

Tip O'Neill
Golf Digest, 1981

It's one of those years. Jimmy Carter had four of 'em, so I don't feel so bad.

Lee Trevino, having a bad year, 1981

The other day my golf-loving friend Bob Hope asked me what my handicap was, so I told him—the Congress.

Ronald Reagan, 1982

Golf, a game kings and presidents play when they get tired of running countries.

Charles Price
Golf Magazine, 1982

Golf, in my opinion, is a game for deposed Latin American dictators in plaid pants; it allows them to putter away their exile until God's extradition.

John Leonard
New York Times, 1982

President Ford waits until he hits his first drive to know what course he's playing that day.

Bob Hope
San Francisco Chronicle, 1983

When Andrei Gromyko gets down to disarmament talks, the first item on his agenda is taking away Gerald Ford's golf clubs.

Bob Hope, 1984

He doesn't know he can't hit the ball through the trunk of a tree.

Jack Nicklaus, on Ford, 1984

The difference between golf and government is that in golf you can't improve your lie.

George Deukmejian, Governor of California
Golf Digest, 1984

17. Hazards

There are no bunkers in the air.

Walter Hagen, on why he hits the ball high, 1920

The object of a bunker or trap is not only to punish a physical mistake, to punish lack of control, but also to punish pride and egotism.

Charles Blair Macdonald, golf course architect
The American Golfer, 1924

Did I make it look hard enough, son?

Walter Hagen, to Norman von Nida after hitting out of the rough to the green, 1929

The difference between a sand trap and water is the difference between a car crash and an airplane crash. You have a chance of recovering from a car crash.

Bobby Jones

Jimmy Demaret lit up whenever it started blowing. I think he was born in the wind. His mother had to run five miles to retrieve him.

Bob Hope, 1953

When they start hitting back at me, it's time to quit.

Henry Ransom, when his shot from the beach at Cypress Point's sixteenth hole rebounded from the cliff and hit him in the stomach, c. 1955

And don't send your Son down. This is a man's job.

> **Bernard Darwin, golf writer, swearing to God**
> **in a bunker**

I've lost balls in every hazard and on every course on which I've tried, but when I lose a ball in the ball washer it's time to take stock.

> **Milton Gross**
> *Eighteen Holes in My Head,* 1959

If the tree is skinny, aim right at it. A peculiarity of golf is that what you aim at you generally miss, . . . the success of the shot depending mainly, of course, on your definition of "skinny."

> **Rex Lardner**
> *Out of the Bunker and Into the Trees,* 1960

If he takes the option of dropping behind the point where the ball rests, keeping in line with the pin, his nearest drop is Honolulu.

> **Jimmy Demaret, on Arnold Palmer on the rocks at**
> **the seventeenth hole at Pebble Beach, 1964**

Hey, is this room out-of-bounds?

> **Alex Karras, after hitting his tee shot through the**
> **clubhouse window at Red Run Country Club,**
> **Royal Oak, Michigan**

Only bullfighting and the water hole are left as vestigial evidence of what a bloody savage man used to be. Only in golf is this sort of contrived swindle allowed.

> **Tommy Bolt**
> *How to Keep Your Temper on the Golf Course,* 1969

The last time I left the fairway was to answer the telephone. And it was a wrong number.
Chi Chi Rodriguez, 1970

What's over there? A nudist colony?
Lee Trevino, after his three playing partners drove into the woods, 1970

Water creates a neurosis in golfers. The very thought of this harmless fluid robs them of their normal powers of rational thought, turns their legs to jelly, and produces a palsy of the upper limbs.
Peter Dobereiner
The Glorious World of Golf, 1973

I spent so much time in the rough, my playing partner Buddy Allin thought I was part of the gallery. I walked so much I had to replace my cleats.
Lee Trevino, at the U.S. Open, 1974

The sand was heavier than I thought, and it only took me four swings to figure it out.
Johnny Miller, at the U.S. Open, 1974

It is not unusual to find strange objects in municipal sand traps, even bones. Some players think that the rake by the side of the trap is a hazard itself and that it is a two-stroke penalty if you touch it.
Jay Cronley
Golf Digest

The number one thing in trouble is: Don't get into more trouble!
Dave Stockton
Golf Magazine, 1977

Check the diaper; if it's wet you get relief from casual water.
**Bob Murphy, when his partner's ball landed in a
baby carriage**
Golf Digest, 1978

I have discovered one important thing about the course,
though—those big pine trees don't move.
Fuzzy Zoeller, at The Masters
Des Moines Register, 1979

I didn't realize how windy it was yesterday until I came out
today and got a look at Tom Watson. The wind had blown
fourteen freckles off Tom's face. Now man, that's windy.
Jerry McGee, at the Andy Williams–San Diego Open
Golf Digest, 1979

A rough should have high grass. When you go bowling they
don't give you anything for landing in the gutter, do they?
Lee Trevino
Golf Digest, 1979

I love rotten weather. The founders of the game accepted
nature for what it gave, or what it took away. Wind and rain
are great challenges. They separate real golfers. Let the seas
pound against the shore, let the rains pour.
Tom Watson
San Francisco Chronicle, 1981

If this was an airport, it would have been closed.
Larry Ziegler, on a windy and rainy day
Golf Magazine, 1982

I've joked about how I survived being struck by lightning. "I'm
a reject," I said. "The Lord didn't want me."
Lee Trevino
They Call Me Super Mex, 1982

I'm too young to get fried up out here—I don't like the game that much.

Fuzzy Zoeller, walking off the course during a thunderstorm, 1983

Golf is the strangest game in the world. It involves a lot of luck. And when your ball starts rattling in the trees, then it's all luck.

Rex Caldwell
San Francisco Chronicle, 1983

My Turn-Ons: big galleries, small scores, long drives, short rough, fat paychecks, and skinny trees.

Peter Jacobsen
Golf Magazine, 1983

They say that trees are no problem because trees are ninety percent air.

John Brodie
"Women's Kemper Open," NBC-TV, 1983

I didn't get much tan this week.

Steve Melnyk, playing in the trees
"Colonial National Invitation," NBC-TV, 1983

My tournament lineup would include . . . any guy who never got out of a sand trap in fewer than six strokes.

Jim Murray
Los Angeles Times, 1983

The wind was so strong there were whitecaps in the porta-john.

Joyce Kazmierski
"Women's Kemper Open," NBC-TV, 1983

Guys from Texas and Florida usually are good wind players. Californians? We're good at buying Mercedeses and ordering dinner at expensive restaurants.

> **Gary McCord**
> *Golf Digest,* 1984

Could you enlighten me as to what crazed Luther Burbank was thinking when he planted that tree by the third hole? A *tree,* for God's sake. Trees belong in the National Arboretum. They have absolutely no place on a golf course.

> **Peter Andrews**
> *Golf Digest,* 1984

I never saw a good player from the trees.

> **Byron Nelson**
> "Doral–Eastern Open," CBS-TV, 1984

On the scenic and infamous par-five eighteenth, he had one last chance, but from the way he struck his tee shot it appeared as if he were trying to hit the ocean in regulation.

> **Dan Jenkins, on Crosby winner Hale Irwin's shot that bounced off the rocks and back on the fairway at Pebble Beach, 1984**

It's only my career, folks.

> **Fuzzy Zoeller, to spectators at the U.S. Open when he was in trouble**
> *Sports Illustrated,* 1984

18. The Majors

British Open

Their only fault is that they give no possible excuse for a missed putt.

> **Bobby Jones, on the greens at Hoylake, England, 1930**

I should have played that hole in an ambulance.

> **Arnold Palmer, on his ten strokes at the seventeenth hole at St. Andrews, 1960**

What did I want with prestige? The British Open paid the winner $600 in American money. A man would have to be two hundred years old at that rate to retire from golf.

> **Sam Snead, on why he hesitated going to Scotland in 1946**
> *The Education of a Golfer, 1962*

I thought I'd blown it at the seventeenth green when I drove into a trap. God is a Mexican.

> **Lee Trevino, eventual winner at Muirfield, Scotland, 1972**

How do you do, Mr. Prime Minister—ever shake hands with a Mexican before?

> **Lee Trevino, meeting British Prime Minister Edward Heath**
> *Sport, 1978*

The winner, Severiano Ballesteros, chose not to use the course but preferred his own, which mainly consisted of hay fields, car parks, grandstands, dropping zones and even ladies' clothing.

Colin Maclaine, Chairman of the Championship Committee, 1979

When Ballesteros triumphed at the British Open in 1979, for his first major win, he hit so few fairways off the tee that he was often mistaken for a gallery marshall.

Dan Jenkins
Sports Illustrated, 1983

All my life I wanted to play golf like Jack Nicklaus, and now I do.

Paul Harvey, news commentator, after Jack Nicklaus shot an eighty-three at Royal St. George's, England, 1981

I'm a serious contender this week. How can they beat me? I've been struck by lightning, had two back operations and been divorced twice.

Lee Trevino, at Royal Birkdale, England
Sports Illustrated, 1983

The Masters

I'll be back every year, if I have to walk fifteen hundred miles to do it.

Herman Keiser, upon winning The Masters, 1946

I'm a stupid. I just signed a wrong card. . . . But I congratulate Bob Goalby, he gave me so much pressure that I lose my brain.

Roberto de Vicenzo, who signed for a four instead of a three for the seventeenth hole, losing The Masters by one shot, 1968

I think maybe I make a few friends. That means more than money. What is money, anyway?

> **Roberto de Vicenzo, on losing The Masters**
> *The Observer* (London), 1968

When [Clifford] Roberts had first asked the show's sponsors . . . for fewer commercials, an agency man in New York had said, "What does he think The Masters is, a moon shot?" The answer was no. Clifford Roberts thought The Masters was infinitely more important than that.

> **Dan Jenkins**
> *The Dogged Victims of Inexorable Fate*, 1970

This is the only course I know where you choke when you come in the gate.

> **Lionel Hebert, 1970**

You can lick this course with your normal game—if you ever calm down enough to play your normal game.

> **Frank Beard**
> *Pro*, 1970

Here's your headline for a picture of that: *Casper to Knees: Lord Says No.*

> **George Archer, as Billy Casper missed a putt at the eighteenth hole for an outright win, 1970**

On the fifteenth hole I had started thinking about the green jacket. They gave it to Charles Coody.

> **Johnny Miller, finishing second, 1971**

The tournament brass will stop at nothing to keep Palmer happy. There is a story that he left the eleventh fairway one year to go into the woods and relieve himself. The next year a permanent restroom had been built on the spot.

> **Dave Hill**
> *Teed Off*, 1977

The Masters is Scarborough Fair, the gathering of eagles. Everyone wants to make the trip to Mecca.

Bob Jones, Jr., son of Robert Trent Jones
Golf Digest, 1978

Green grass, green grandstands, green concession stalls, green paper cups, green folding chairs and visors for sale, green-and-white ropes, green-topped Georgia pines . . . If justice were poetic, Hubert Green would win it every year.

John Updike
"Thirteen Ways of Looking at The Masters," 1980

The reason I always watch The Masters is to see if it's really true that a bird has never crapped on that golf course.

Jay Cronley
Playboy, 1981

Reporter: Exactly what size is that jacket?
Stadler: I don't know, and I'm not about to take it off and find out.

Craig Stadler, Masters champion, 1982

My, even the fairways are fast!

Byron Nelson, playing an exhibition before The Masters
The New Yorker, 1982

If you don't get an invitation, it's like being out of the world a whole week.

Doug Ford
San Francisco Examiner, 1982

The Masters is more like a vast Edwardian garden party than a golf tournament.

Alistair Cooke
TV Guide, 1983

If you didn't know better, six hours of The Masters on CBS could leave you with the feeling that Augusta National Golf Club is a holy land and the winner of the tournament will be passing through a corridor where no mere mortal will ever tread.

> Tom Gilmore
> *San Francisco Chronicle,* 1984

Professional Golfers Association Championship

He may have gone to bed three hours ago. But he knows who he is playing. You can rest assured that he hasn't slept a wink.

> **Walter Hagen, on his match-play opponent, 1919**

I guess I was just plain scared to win that dude.

> **Don January, after losing in a playoff to Jerry Barber, 1961**

Another weekend with nothing to do.

> **Arnold Palmer, after missing the cut**
> *Golf Digest,* 1978

The crowd was mumbling about Nicklaus, but I didn't need them to tell me that the Bear was coming.

> **Hal Sutton, holding off Nicklaus to win**
> *Sports Illustrated,* 1983

United States Open Championship

Any player can win a U.S. Open, but it takes a helluva player to win two.

> **Walter Hagen**

I can't see why I broke so badly. Why, I am sure I could go out now and do better by kicking the ball around with my boot.

> **Harry Vardon, on his seventy-eight in the final round, 1920**

Nobody wins the Open. It wins you.

> **Dr. Cary Middlecoff**

Palmer: Doesn't 280 always win the Open?
Jenkins: Yeah, when Hogan shoots it.

> **Arnold Palmer and Dan Jenkins, sportswriter, at Cherry Hills, 1960**

I may buy the Alamo and give it back to Mexico.

> **Lee Trevino, asked what he'd do with the winnings, 1968**

Well, I'm not gonna buy this place. It doesn't have indoor plumbing.

> **Lee Trevino, after going to San Antonio and seeing the Alamo, 1968**

It was like unhitching a horse from a plow and winning the Kentucky Derby, or a guy stepping out of the audience, removing his coat and knocking out the heavyweight champion of the world.

> **Jim Murray, on unheralded Orville Moody winning the U.S. Open**
> *Los Angeles Times,* 1969

What does it matter who Orville Moody is? At least he brought the title back to America.

> **Dave Marr, on Moody succeeding Lee Trevino as the U.S. Open champion, 1969**

Another writer asked me what I thought the course needed and I said eighty acres of corn and a few cows. I borrowed that crack from Bob Rosburg.

Dave Hill, on Hazeltine Golf Club, site of the 1970 U.S. Open

When I was walking down the fairway, I saw a bunch of USGA guys down on their hands and knees parting the rough trying to find my ball. I knew I was in trouble.

Jim Colbert, on the U.S. Open at Winged Foot Golf Club, 1974

Putting these greens is like walking on titties.

Homero Blancas, on Winged Foot, 1974

It couldn't have been too bad a lie. I could still see your knees.

Hubert Green, to Lanny Wadkins at Winged Foot, 1974

The fringe around the greens isn't fringe at all but long grass. . . . The scrambler is better off back home eating beer nuts and watching it on TV.

Dan Gleason, on U.S. Open courses
The Great, The Grand and the Also-Ran, 1976

All of a sudden I'm an expert on everything. Interviewers want your opinion of golf, foreign policy and even the price of peanuts.

Hubert Green, upon winning the Open, 1977

He played almost the entire final round without putting his spikes to a fairway. He spent so much time in sand that if you held his wedge to your ear, you could hear the ocean.

> **Joe Gergen, on J.C. Snead, who finished second in the Open at Cherry Hills Country Club**
> *Newsday*, 1978

I was so charged up I couldn't turn my engine off. I think this may have had something to do with the fact that I ran out of gas on the second nine today. I was operating just on vapor.

> **Hale Irwin, after winning the Open at Inverness**
> *The New Yorker*, 1979

That's the way it is at the U.S. Open golf tournament. Whoever's in the lead feels like the first guy onto the beach at Normandy on D-day.

> **Gary Nuhn**
> Dayton *Daily News*, 1979

There's really not much to do. We're just mowing the greens and letting the rough grow. When it gets so that only a couple of guys on our staff can break eighty it will be ready.

> **Steve McLennan, head pro, Pebble Beach, preparing the course for the Open, 1982**

Watson is doing to Nicklaus what Nicklaus was doing to me twenty years ago. I knew exactly what Nicklaus was thinking when Watson's chip went in.

> **Arnold Palmer, on Tom Watson's winning chip shot at the seventeenth hole at Pebble Beach to win the Open, 1982**

That took all the wind out of my sails and I just really never had a chance to get much going the rest of the year. It doesn't often happen with a shot by somebody else; you usually do it to yourself.

> **Jack Nicklaus, on Watson's chip**
> *Golf Digest*, 1983

When I saw Jack Nicklaus hit some shots out of it sideways yesterday, I was convinced it was tough.

> **Lanny Wadkins, on the rough at Oakmont Country Club**
> *San Francisco Chronicle,* 1983

The U.S. Open flag eliminates a lot of players. Some players just weren't meant to win the U.S. Open. Quite often, a lot of them know it.

> **Jack Nicklaus**
> *Golf Digest,* 1983

We're not trying to humiliate the greatest players in the world. We're trying to identify them.

> **Frank Tatum, former USGA president, on the tough conditions of the U.S. Open courses**
> *Sports Illustrated,* 1984

19. Match Play

Do not allow yourself to be annoyed because your opponent insists on making elaborate study of all his putts.

> **Horace G. Hutchinson**
> *Hints on the Game of Golf,* 1886

A secret disbelief in the enemy's play is very useful for match play.

> **Sir Walter Simpson**
> *The Art of Golf,* 1887

A golf course exists primarily for match play, which is a sport, as distinguished from stroke play, which more resembles rifle shooting than a sport in that it lacks the joy of personal contact with an opponent.
Freddie Tait, British professional, c. 1890s

A good player who is a great putter is a match for any golfer. A great hitter who cannot putt is a match for no one.
Ben Sayers, Scottish professional, c. 1890s

This made him two up and three to play. What an average golfer would consider a commanding lead. But Archibald was no average golfer. A commanding lead for him would have been two up and one to play.
P. G. Wodehouse
"Archibald's Benefit," 1919

You know, Sam, man still is a primitive being. Let someone betray a weakness and he's ready for the kill.
Freddie Martin, West Virginia professional, advice to Sam Snead, 1936

I can beat any two players in this tournament by myself. If I need any help, I'll let you know.
Babe Didrikson Zaharias, to her partner Peggy Kirk Bell in a four-ball event

We're five up now, but what's wrong with winning by eight or ten?
Ben Hogan, at the Inverness Four-Ball tournament, to partner Jimmy Demaret, 1941

Reporter: What was the turning point, Jimmy?
Demaret: When I teed off at ten o'clock.
Jimmy Demaret, on losing to Ben Hogan ten-and-eight at the PGA Championship in Portland, 1946

My father was thinking of coming out for this tournament. Then when he found out who I had drawn as my first opponent, he changed his mind. He decided it wasn't worth a trip to Colorado just to watch me play one round.

Robert T. Jones III, son of Bobby Jones, on being matched against Jack Nicklaus in the National Amateur Championship, 1959

If you keep shooting par at them, they all crack sooner or later.

Bobby Jones

I have found, in my own matches, that if you just keep throwing consistent, unvarying bogeys and double bogeys at your opponents, they will crack up sooner or later from the pressure.

Rex Lardner
Out of the Bunker and Into the Trees, 1960

I had held a notion that I could make a pretty fair appraisal of the worth of an opponent simply by speaking to him on the first tee and taking a good measuring look into his eyes.

Bobby Jones
Golf Is My Game, 1960

Over the years, I've studied habits of golfers. I know what to look for. Watch their eyes. Fear shows up when there is an enlargement of the pupils. Big pupils lead to big scores.

Sam Snead

No matter what happens—*never give up a hole.* . . . In tossing in your cards after a bad beginning you also undermine your whole game, because to quit between tee and green is more habit-forming than drinking a highball before breakfast.

Sam Snead
The Education of a Golfer, 1962

Everyone gets wounded in a game of golf. The trick is not to bleed.

> **Peter Dobereiner**
> *The Observer* (London), 1967

Match play, you see, is much more of a joust. It calls for a doughty, resourceful competitor, the sort of fellow who is not ruffled by his opponent's fireworks and is able to set off a few of his own when it counts.

> **Herbert Warren Wind**
> *Golf Digest,* 1972

Stroke play is a better test of golf, but match play is a better test of character.

> **Joe Carr, Irish amateur**

20. Media

You could have shot off an elephant gun in my corner of the locker room and not winged a single sportswriter.

> **Sam Snead, recalling when he finished second as a rookie in the U.S. Open in 1937**

Announcer: This is the big one, folks. . . . Now he's sighting the putt. . . . Now he's bending over and addressing the ball. . . . Now he's glaring in my direction.

> **Robert Day, cartoon**
> *The New Yorker,* 1950

Sam Snead won The Masters yesterday on greens that were slicker than the top of his head.

> **Dan Jenkins, proposed lead**
> Fort Worth *Press,* 1952

He's hit it fat. . . . It will probably be short. . . . It just hit the front edge of the green. . . . It's got no chance. . . . It's rolling but it will stop. . . . It's rolling toward the cup. . . . Well I'll be damned!

Jimmy Demaret, commenting on television on Lew Worsham's winning wedge shot at the World Championship, 1953

So many of my golfing pals have been punching a typewriter between tournament dates that an awful lot of people were beginning to stare at me, wondering what was wrong. "Do you think he's illiterate?" I heard one fellow whisper behind my back.

Jimmy Demaret
My Partner, Ben Hogan, 1954

If someone dropped an atom bomb on the sixth hole, the press would wait for a golfer to come in and tell them about it.

Ben Hogan

Q: Have you noticed much difference between the various courses you've seen on television?
A: Not much. All of them seem to have "one of the greatest finishing holes in golf."

Frank Hannigan, USGA official
USGA Golf Journal, 1964

The eighteenth, . . . one of the great finishing holes in golf.

Pat Summerall
"Colonial National Invitation," CBS-TV, 1984

Cut your talk in half. You're not saying anything interesting, anyhow.

Frank Chirkinian, CBS-TV producer, to his commentators at The Masters, 1966

They [the press] do an excellent job considering the fact that they're writing about something about which they know nothing.

> **Frank Beard, paraphrasing jockey Bill Hartack**
> *Pro,* 1970

Even the announcers are choking.

> **Tony Jacklin, on the CBS crew covering**
> **The Masters, 1970**

If only I had taken up golf earlier and devoted my whole time to it instead of fooling about writing stories and things, I might have got my handicap down to under eighteen.

> **P. G. Wodehouse**
> *The Golf Omnibus,* 1973

The professional golf watcher never catches the action. I could write a volume on Great Moments in Golf I Have Missed.

> **Peter Dobereiner**
> *The Glorious World of Golf,* 1973

Lie? I've got no f——ing lie. I don't even have a f——ing shot.

> **Miller Barber, when asked by Ken Venturi about**
> **his lie on the CBS Golf Classic**

As I said in the press tent, "Man, I crawled on that shot like an eight-wheel rig rollin' down Interstate 35. Just wore it out. And the minute the ball started for that flagstick I knew the war was over and it was time to call in the boats and piss on the admiral."

> **Dan Jenkins**
> *Dead Solid Perfect,* 1974

Writers are very strict about touring pros having familiar names. Editors make writers take laps and do pushups when Jack Fleck or Orville Moody wins a U.S. Open.

Dan Jenkins
Golf Digest, 1975

Chris, the boys are hitting the ball longer now because they're getting more distance.

Byron Nelson, to Chris Schenkel on ABC-TV

Lord Byron. ABC's golfing colorman who pioneered the phrase, "That's right, Chris."

Mark Mulvoy and Art Spander
Golf: The Passion and the Challenge, 1977

Sports ratings are totally affected by the weather. If I have a major sports telecast coming up, I literally go home at night and pray for terrible weather.

Don Ohlmeyer, NBC Sports golf producer
Golf Digest, 1979

Nancy Lopez is planning to marry a sportscaster. I thought she had better taste.

Dick Schaap
Sport, 1979

"I do not read papers," Leon said. "I look at the golf scores and then I wrap fish in them."

Dan Gleason
Golf Digest, 1981

Looking back today, I can think of no surer way to find yourself a golf writer in your fifties than to think you were Ben Hogan in your twenties.

Charles Price
Golfer-At-Large, 1982

ABC is star-oriented. They would rather watch Nicklaus walk than another player strike a golf shot.

Frank Chirkinian, CBS-TV golf producer
Sports Illustrated, 1982

Wright whispered, "And it appears that, at last, the great man is going to strike his tiny spheroid; and will it find its way into that marvelous pit or will it stay, like a rebellious child, at the entrance and refuse to go in?"

Kevin Cook, parodying golf announcer Ben Wright
Playboy, 1982

It is still disappointingly cool here for those who like to witness the female form.

Ben Wright
"Colonial National Invitation," CBS-TV, 1983

The average golfer would rather play than watch. Those who don't play can't possibly appreciate the subleties of the game. Trying to get their attention with golf is like selling Shakespeare in the neighborhood saloon.

Bob Toski
The Sporting News, 1983

Peter Jacobsen is in a position where a birdie will help him more than a bogey.

Steve Melnyk
"Colonial National Invitation," CBS-TV, 1983

I'm really going to do my homework. . . . I'm going to be down there on the practice tee before the telecast, finding out if a guy's wife beat him up the night before. Important stuff like that. Stuff that people want to know.

Lee Trevino, on his new job as TV golf commentator
Golf Digest, 1983

I don't mind that booth. That's pretty good money. I almost finish third every week I'm up there.

Lee Trevino
New York Times, 1984

My job on the telecasts was relatively easy. I would sit up on a tower behind a green and try to guess which sets of tits in the gallery were following which golfers.

Dan Jenkins
Life Its Ownself, 1984

I was afraid to move my lips in front of TV. The Commissioner probably would have fined me just for what I was thinking.

Tom Weiskopf, on his thirteen in the 1980 Masters
San Francisco Chronicle, 1984

No one can misquote me, because they don't know what the hell I'm talking about.

Gary McCord, known as "Space Cadet"
San Jose Mercury News, 1984

The cameras affect my game. They make me nervous. I would rather make my money in front of nobody.

Betsy King
Golf Digest, 1984

There is one thing in this world that is dumber than playing golf. That is watching someone else play golf. . . . What do you actually get to see? Thirty-seven guys in polyester slacks squinting at the sun. Doesn't that set your blood racing?

Peter Andrews
Golf Digest, 1984

Watching The Masters on CBS is like attending a church service. Announcers speak in hushed, pious tones, as if to convince us that something of great meaning and historical importance is taking place. What we are actually seeing is grown men hitting little balls with sticks.

> **Tom Gilmore**
> *San Francisco Chronicle,* 1984

Well, the Real Leader keeps sending us messages.

> **Pat Summerall, when lightning struck**
> **"The Masters," CBS-TV, 1984**

I've been here since 1968, and I cry every time.

> **Pat Summerall, as leader Ben Crenshaw came up**
> **the eighteenth fairway**
> **"The Masters," CBS-TV, 1984**

21. Men's Tour

I've just discovered the great secret of golf. You can't play a really hot game unless you're so miserable that you don't worry over your shots . . . Look at the top-notchers. Have you ever seen a happy pro?

> **P. G. Wodehouse**
> "The Heart of a Goof," 1923

Why shouldn't he? He's never done anything all his life but play golf.

> **Mr. Turnesa, upon hearing that his son, Joe, was**
> **leading the U.S. Open, 1926**

There are two kinds of golf—golf and tournament golf. The latter is an aging game.

Bobby Jones, 1930

Golf championships are a good deal like omelets. You cannot have an omelet without breaking eggs, and you cannot have a golf championship without wrecking hopes.

O. B. Keeler, biographer of Bobby Jones

Not really. After all, I put it there.

Walter Hagen, when a spectator mentioned the bad luck of his lie

I think I missed the cut—if I teed off at all. I forget. In those days, me and Clayton Heafner had a bad habit of being withdrew.

George Low, on the 1939 British Open

I guess I've traveled a hundred thousand miles a year on the pro tour, but the only thing of interest I've ever seen is the Washington Monument.

Don Whitt, c. 1950s

Life on the Tournament Trail. The Road to Psychiatry.

Jimmy Demaret, chapter heading
My Partner, Ben Hogan, 1954

The players themselves can be classified roughly into two groups—the attractions and the entry fees.

Jimmy Demaret
My Partner, Ben Hogan, 1954

I have never felt so lonely as on a golf course in the midst of a championship with thousands of people around, especially when things began to go wrong and the crowds started wandering away.

> **Bobby Jones**
> *Golf Is My Game,* 1960

Some of the things I didn't have to be taught as a rookie traveling pro were to keep close count of my nickels and dimes, stay away from whiskey, and never concede a putt.

> **Sam Snead**
> *The Education of a Golfer,* 1962

Don't get excited, Flick. Even a stopped clock is right twice a day.

> **Peter Kostis, to fellow pro Jim Flick after an ace**

A golf professional is a fellow who never knows what town he's in till he calls downstairs to the desk clerk in the morning, . . . but can read you the left-to-right break on every green in the town from memory.

> **Jim Murray**
> *The Sporting World of Jim Murray,* 1968

Out here, you've got to realize that if you take an eight on a hole, ninety percent of the other pros don't care and the other ten percent wish it had been a nine.

> **Mason Rudolph, at the Tucson Open, 1969**

What golf needs is a fist-fight between Jack Nicklaus and Arnold Palmer on the eighteenth green of a nationally televised tournament.

> **Jean Shepard, humorist**

What do I like about all this besides the money? This is my office, and I love my office.

> **Chi Chi Rodriguez, waving at the fairways**
> *Playboy,* 1970

The men's tour was quiet, after all. Terry Dill wouldn't be changing his grip for another week or so. Dick Lotz still had the same putter. Bert Yancey had postponed his annual interview until July.

> **Dan Jenkins**
> *Sports Illustrated,* 1971

There's an old saying on tour, "Set fire to the tees and cover the greens with broken glass, put the pros out there in gasoline-soaked pants and barefooted, and someone will break par."

> **Tommy Bolt**
> *The Hole Truth,* 1971

I've decided to have a tournament of my own, called the Flip Wilson Ghetto Open. Bob, I know your tournament is played to benefit the Eisenhower Memorial Hospital, mine will be played for the Richard Pryor Clinic for Rat Bites and Bullet Wounds.

> **Flip Wilson, to Bob Hope**
> "The Flip Wilson Show," NBC-TV, 1971

I never knew what top golf was like until I turned professional—then it was too late.

> **Steve Melnyk, former U.S. Amateur champion, 1973**

The amateur who picks up his newspaper and remarks that he could shoot better golf than those guys on tour should pause and consider the prospects very carefully . . . It is not just a different game. It is not a game at all.

> **Peter Dobereiner**
> *The Glorious World of Golf,* 1973

In the past, I've usually played in about thirty-five tournaments a year, but I played so poorly last year that I didn't have the courage to leave home.

Steve Reid
Golf Digest, 1973

About July, the steak in St. Louis looks like the same one you had in Los Angeles. Don't talk about the potatoes and peas.

Charles Coody, 1973

Before Arnold Palmer came along the only guys on the tour were a bunch of dull bastards.

Herb Graffis, golf writer and editor

Wife: Have you gotten to know many of the players?
Bev: Are you kidding? How do you talk to an Amana hat?

Dan Jenkins
Dead Solid Perfect, 1974

If you were a golf pro, I decided, whether you were good enough to play the tour or not, it wouldn't matter if the damned old sun didn't rise. You could just reach up and switch on the light.

Dan Jenkins
Dead Solid Perfect, 1974

Every time a circus leaves town, there are people who'd like to leave with it. A lot of waitresses who've overheard the tour talk sigh and go back to eggs-over and the humdrum of soap operas.

Dan Gleason
The Great, The Grand and the Also-Ran, 1976

If backing a Broadway play is the worst investment in the world, sponsoring a pro golfer surely ranks a strong second.

Mark Mulvoy and Art Spander
Golf: The Passion and the Challenge, 1977

If you travel first class, you think first class and you're more
likely to play first class.
>   **Raymond Floyd, on why his tour expenses are**
>   **$60,000 a year, 1977**

It's a compromise of what your ego wants you to do, what
experience tells you to do, and what your nerves let you do.
>   **Bruce Crampton, on tournament golf**

Only religious ceremonies proceed with more respect than the
major golf tournaments in this country.
>   **Jimmy Cannon**
>   *Nobody Asked Me, But . . .* , 1978

Resolve this thought in your mind. . . . Arnold Palmer might
be the greatest golfer in the world, but he probably doesn't
know a carburetor from a tail pipe.
>   **Dan Jenkins**
>   *Golf Digest,* 1979

To be in contention for three or four days is better than stick-
ing a needle in the arm.
>   **David Graham**
>   *San Francisco Chronicle,* 1981

Most of us would give up our wives, our firstborn and our
favorite putters just to finish in the top ten in a major.
>   **Lee Trevino**
>   *San Jose Mercury News,* 1981

To be a successful tour golfer you have to hate everybody,
your mom and dad, your wife, your children, your brothers
and sisters, your friends—everybody. It takes total concentration, and I mean total.
>   **Dave Hill**
>   *Golf Digest,* 1982

The only positive thing to come out of losing my exemption is that I found out who my friends are. I thought I had a million friends when I was playing well, but I've learned that I have damn few.

Frank Beard
Golf Magazine, 1981

Sam Snead: If I putted like Jack Nicklaus, I'd have won a thousand tournaments.
Tommy Bolt: If Jack played in as many tournaments as you, he'd have won two thousand.

Tommy Bolt and Sam Snead
Golf Digest, 1981

If you call personality the battle of Hollywood stars, then, yes, we do lack personality. But the personality of golf is good golf. If you want to see a comedian, you ought to tune in "Saturday Night Live."

Tom Watson
The Sporting News, 1982

I can't believe the actions of some of our top pros. They should have side jobs modeling for Pampers.

Fuzzy Zoeller
Golf Digest, 1982

Golf, especially championship golf, isn't supposed to be any fun, was never meant to be fair, and never will make any sense.

Charles Price
Golfer-At-Large, 1982

My luck is so bad that if I bought a cemetery, people would stop dying.

Ed Furgol
Golf Magazine, 1982

During the last hour and a half of play on this round, when the heat of the sun had diminished, we had one of those stretches when watching expert golfers in action seems like one of the high-ranking blessings of life.

Herbert Warren Wind, on the U.S. Open at Oakmont
The New Yorker, 1983

The job of a finishing hole is as clearly defined as that of a dance hall bouncer. It has to maintain order, clear out the amateurs, preserve the dignity of the game.

Jim Murray
Golf Magazine, 1983

More money. Otherwise, no difference. Birdie the same. Par the same. Bogey the same. Out-of-bounds the same.

Seve Ballesteros, on the difference between the Tour and the rest of the world
Golf Magazine, 1983

Next the Golf Journeyman's Union will put in belly dancers, the tattooed lady and JoJo the dog-faced boy to make more money and degrade a sport that was once distinguished by class.

Herb Graffis, golf writer, on the commercialization of the PGA Tour
Golf Digest, 1983

A bad week on the Tour is when the demons dance through your swing thoughts. In the real world a bad week is when you wake up to find you're a steelworker in Youngstown.

Don Wade
Golf Digest, 1983

Golf seemed so easy then. Then you grow up and learn to weep.

Ron Rhoads, on golf as a youngster compared to the life of a professional
65th PGA Championship program, 1983

I'm so busy I can only play in one tournament at a time.

Jack Nicklaus
Golf Digest, 1983

I'd rather work in a 7–11 store than go back to playing the mini-tour.

Kenny Knox
Golf Digest, 1983

You have to take this game through so many labyrinths of the mind, past all the traps—like, will my masculinity be threatened if I hit the ball well and still shoot seventy-two?

Mac O'Grady
Sports Illustrated, 1984

Sometimes you'd like to just stand there in the middle of the green and scream as loud as you can. But we're the perfect gentlemen.

Raymond Floyd
Golf Magazine, 1984

The trouble with this game is that they say the good breaks and bad breaks even up. What they don't tell you is that they don't even up right away. You might go two or three years and all you get is bad break-bad break-bad break. That gets annoying in a hurry.

Johnny Miller
Golf Magazine, 1984

22. Modern Days/Olden Days

I noticed a lady in the clubhouse at the weekend. I urge the Secretary to see that this does not happen again.

Entry in complaints register, Worcestershire Golf Club, England, 1881

The professional, as we are now chiefly acquainted with him, is a feckless, reckless creature. In the golfing season in Scotland he makes his money all the day, and spends it all the night. His sole loves are golf and whiskey.

Horace G. Hutchinson, golf historian, 1900

For that kind of money, I'd wear a skirt.

Jimmy Demaret, on the prize money of the 1930s, when asked to wear a number on his back

Play is conducted at a snail's pace. Some golfers today remind me of kids walking to school and praying they'll be late . . . Golfers used to check the grass on the greens; today they study the roots under each blade.

Jimmy Demaret
My Partner, Ben Hogan, 1954

Q: When and how did golf begin?
A: Arnold Palmer invented it about eight years ago in a little town outside Pittsburgh.

Frank Hannigan, USGA official
USGA Golf Journal, 1964

All you got out there is a bunch of authors and haberdashers. All you got to do to write a book is win one tournament. All of a sudden you're telling everybody where the V's ought to point. And them that don't win, they're haberdashers. They sell sweaters and slacks and call themselves pros.

George Low, former touring professional, c. 1960s

I've noticed some of them are off balance when they swing. They're top-heavy. They've got too much hair.

Ben Hogan, on today's golfers
Golf Digest, 1970

These kids have it mighty soft today. I recently heard one of my members say to his son: "You're a golf bum. Are you going to be content to spend your life tramping around the golf course?" And the kid said, "No, Pop, I've been meaning to speak to you about buying me my own golf cart."

Sam Snead
Golf Magazine, 1970

I just love to see you guys with long hair, because you can't see. I never saw a hippie playing golf.

Bert Yancey, c. early 1970s

Hickory golf was a game of manipulation and inspiration; steel golf is a game of precision and calculation.

Peter Dobereiner
The Glorious World of Golf, 1973

We always considered it quite a feat to get down our six-to-eight footers, but now if a fellow misses from forty feet he grimaces and agonizes like a cowboy struck in the heart by an Indian's arrow.

Ben Hogan
Sports Illustrated, 1973

Those young amateurs who join the tour remind me of young horses that have raced too much too soon. They're burned out before they get to the big races. Then they have to go back to the paddock and learn all over again.

Chi Chi Rodriguez
Golf Digest, 1975

Man, I've got to blow dry my hair or I've got to withdraw from the tournament. I don't play anywhere unless I can blow dry my hair.

Ben Crenshaw, c. late 1970s

Professional golf has become a game with too much character and not enough characters.

Thomas Boswell
Washington Post, 1979

Palmer and now Nicklaus have been trampled out of sight by these kids nobody has heard of, the colleges down South clone 'em, you can't keep their names straight from one tournament to the next.

John Updike
Rabbit Is Rich, 1981

My God, the courses these kids play today are either half casual water or ground-under-repair. . . . One of these days I'm going to write a book on drops. That ought to sell. The shot's become more popular than putting.

Jimmy Demaret

We didn't have any money but we had some pork and beans and a siphon. That latter implement we called the Oklahoma credit card.

Jimmy Demaret, on golf in the 1930s
Golf Magazine, 1983

There are too many strange faces and computer minds out there these days. You don't even know the people you're playing with.

Billy Casper, cutting back his schedule
Golf Digest, 1983

I come from a different era. I'm from the club era. I started out shining shoes, giving lessons, selling 10E shoes to some guy who wears 12C, and making him like it.

Lee Trevino
USA Today, 1983

There are no short hitters on tour anymore—just long and unbelievably long.

Sam Snead
Golf Digest, 1984

There's so much money, all down the line, that some of 'em don't even drink coffee or a Coke. They say it might make them nervous. Now ain't that something.

Sam Snead
Golf Magazine, 1984

The only thing good about the old days is talking about them.

Bill Melhorn
Golf Secrets Exposed, 1984

23. Money

If you don't mind, Mr. Crosby, I'd rather have cash.

Sam Snead, declining a $500 check for winning the Bing Crosby Pro-Am, 1937

Sam is the only man to make a million dollars and save two million.

Fred Corcoran, Sam Snead's former manager

Try playing for money when you haven't got any.

Lloyd Mangrum

However, 1940, when I won six of nine tournaments, including The Masters, was my big year. I was even able to hang onto enough money so that I needed only a small loan for carfare home.

Jimmy Demaret
My Partner, Ben Hogan, 1954

I never wanted to be a millionaire; I just wanted to live like one.

Walter Hagen
The Walter Hagen Story, 1957

My yearly income averages about $10,000, but I spend $50,000 of my friends' money.

George Low, former touring professional
Golf Digest, 1960

Loaning you money is like sending lettuce by rabbit.

George Low, to Al Besselink

The only pro golfer I would send my laundry to is Chen Ching-po.

Dave Marr, on Arnold Palmer's laundry establishments

One pro said, "Snead's so tight he'd spend his last dollar buying a pocketbook to put it in."

Sam Snead
The Education of a Golfer, 1962

His idea of charity is that it begins—and ends—at home.

> **Jim Murray, on Sam Snead**
> *The Sporting World of Jim Murray,* 1968

Let's see, I think right now, I'm third in money-winning and first in money-spending.

> **Tony Lema, to newsmen at the British Open, 1964**

Did I ever *win* that much before? I never *saw* that much before.

> **Lee Trevino, on winning $6,000 for fourth place at the U.S. Open, 1967**

I'm on steak now. With $200,000 a year, ain't no sense in eating rice and beans any more.

> **Chi Chi Rodriguez, on his weight gain, 1970**

I've always argued that we ought to play right down the middle of Saigon if the price is right.

> **Frank Beard**
> *Pro,* 1970

I'm in the process of looking for a cattle ranch. . . . I keep hearing there's no money in it, but if that were true you couldn't buy a steak.

> **Ben Hogan**
> *Golf Digest,* 1970

Bet you have never heard of a tour player striking because they wouldn't give him weekends off, have you?

> **Tommy Bolt**
> *The Hole Truth,* 1971

Man: One thing is sure. Gene still has every one of those dollars.

Hagen: Hell, he still has the wheelbarrow.

Walter Hagen, on Gene Sarazen, 1972

I'm a good example. Kenny Lee Puckett, white man, thirty-four. Compared to your basic millionaire like Jack Nicklaus, I'm nobody. But I can win myself about $100,000 a year if I can just manage to thump the ball around with my dick.

Dan Jenkins
Dead Solid Perfect, 1974

You know, someday somebody's gonna come out here and tee it up nude.

Bob Wynn, on endorsement money, 1975

I just signed to do commercials for a mattress company and fulfilled my life's ambition. I'll get paid for lying down.

Lee Trevino, 1976

I'll tell you: Julius Boros would be a bookkeeper in Connecticut; Arnold Palmer would still be in the Coast Guard; and I'd be back in Texas picking cotton.

Lee Trevino, on where pro golfers would be without sponsorship money

Every time you win a little prize of some kind, it stimulates you a little bit, if for no other reason than it's one time you didn't get your brains beat out at something.

Dave Marr, 1975

I'm working as hard as I can to get my life and my cash to run out at the same time. If I can just die after lunch Tuesday, everything will be fine.

Doug Sanders
Golf Digest, 1979

The world's a funny place. When you have no money, no one will do anything for you. If you become successful and pile up enough money to buy anything you want, people deluge you with gifts you don't need and try to do all kinds of things for you.

> **Lee Trevino**
> *The New Yorker,* 1980

I owe everything to golf. Where else could a guy with an IQ like mine make this much money?

> **Hubert Green**
> *Sports Illustrated,* 1981

The guys out here are starting to look like race car drivers.

> **Tom Weiskopf, on product logos on clothing and equipment**
> *Golf Digest,* 1981

I made $7,000 on the tour and spent $100,000. The IRS man sent me a get-well card.

> **Chi Chi Rodriguez**
> *USA Today,* 1982

I dropped off the tour and went home and started working with my Dad doing taxes. After two months of that, I decided golf looked pretty good.

> **John Fought**
> "Bob Hope Desert Classic," NBC-TV, 1983

I used to think you had to spend money to make money. This year I'm going to make a lot of money and I'm going to spend *nothing.*

> **Rex Caldwell**
> *Sports Illustrated,* 1983

I'm not concerned about getting in the record books. A good obituary doesn't exactly excite me.
JoAnne Carner
Golf Digest, 1983

What's wrong with being a millionaire? We should all be one.
Terry Diehl
Golf Digest, 1983

I'm going for broke. I was born broke, so I want to live like a millionaire and die poor; I don't want to live poor and die a millionaire.
Chi Chi Rodriguez, at the Everett Open, 1984

My goal is to become filthy rich. But obviously, that isn't going to be in golf. I'm working on a stock-market fraud.
Gary McCord
San Jose Mercury News, 1984

Things were a lot better when I had only one checkbook.
Patty Sheehan
Sports Illustrated, 1984

I still don't think we play for enough money considering how much they make. Everywhere else we play for charity. At the Tournament Players Championship, the purse was $800,000. They make $500,000 on beer.
Lee Trevino
USA Today, 1984

You can make a lot of money in this game. Just ask my ex-wives. Both of them are so rich that neither of their husbands work.
Lee Trevino
USA Today, 1985

I've taken one of those Trevino vacations—five or six weeks off. The tax man is after me.

> Peter Jacobsen
> "Honda Classic," NBC-TV, 1985

24. Nineteenth Hole

Moderation is essential in all things, Madam, but never in my life have I failed to beat a teetotaler.

> **Harry Vardon, when asked to join the temperance movement, c. 1915**

Hell, I don't even get up at that hour to close the window.

> **Walter Hagen, ignoring an early tee time**

I don't drink water because fish f_____ in it.

> **Tommy Armour**

I always keep a supply of stimulants handy in case I see a snake, which I also keep handy.

> **W. C. Fields, putting whiskey in his golf bag**

I like to say I was born on the nineteenth hole—the only one I ever parred.

> **George Low, touring professional**

Me and the pilot got out safe, but the booze died.

> **George Low, on a plane crash**

Geez! I know I was drinking last night, but how did I get to Squaw Valley?

Jimmy Demaret, seeing snow on the fairways at the Bing Crosby Pro-Am, 1962

I saw more than a few pros floating around barrooms at night, trying to kiss the bartender good night because they couldn't tell him from their girlfriends.

Sam Snead
The Education of a Golfer, 1962

Sam was born with a natural ability to keep his bar bills as low as his golf scores.

Jimmy Demaret, on Sam Snead
My Partner, Ben Hogan, 1954

If I try to leave the hotel tonight, put out a contract on me.

Dave Marr, after starting a round with a hangover, 1968

You know what I did here one year? I was so nervous I drank a fifth of rum before I played. I shot the happiest eighty-three of my life.

Chi Chi Rodriguez, at The Masters, 1970

At golf you've got to be mentally alert. You can't lean against a tree that isn't there.

Doug Sanders, on rumors of drugs on the tour, early 1970s

Golfers don't fist fight. They cuss a lot. But they wouldn't punch anything or anybody. They might hurt their hands and have to change their grip.

Dan Jenkins
Dead Solid Perfect, 1974

Reporter: Are you having a party if you win?
Trevino: If I win here Sunday, I won't know it till Thursday.
Lee Trevino, at The Masters, 1978

Baby, I counted fourteen beer bottles in there with your fingerprints on 'em. That must have been some party.
Lee Trevino, to Dave Hill at the World Series of Golf

They're usually pretty red.
Raymond Floyd, when asked the color of his eyes
Golf Digest, 1978

I was in bed at 10 and up at 10:15. Who can sleep at a time like that?
Fuzzy Zoeller, the night before winning the Andy Williams San Diego Open, 1979

I have never led the tour in money winnings, but I have many times in alcohol consumption.
Fuzzy Zoeller
San Francisco Chronicle, 1979

When Jack Nicklaus told me last night I had to play Seve Ballesteros, I took so many pills I'm glad they don't have drug tests for golfers.
Fuzzy Zoeller, at the Ryder Cup
Sports Illustrated, 1983

I admit my personality is to have fun. . . . I've been known to party day and night. Heck, in Las Vegas I paid a guy $50 an hour to sleep for me.
Doug Sanders
San Jose Mercury News, 1984

I asked Jimmy Demaret what was his favorite drink and he said, "The next one."
Phil Harris, commentator
"Legends of Golf," NBC-TV, 1984

Weiskopf: Wouldn't it be great if you could come out here and just pick the tournaments you like to play, never practice, hang out at the bars and have a couple of drinks if you wanted, and just have fun?
Snead: Tom, that's what you've done your whole life.
Tom Weiskopf and J.C. Snead
San Francisco Chronicle, 1984

The way I hit the ball today, I need to go to the range. Instead, I think I'll go to the bar.
Fuzzy Zoeller, at the PGA Championship
USA Today, 1984

25. Philosophy and Advice

Tam Arte Quam Marte: As much by skill as by strength.
Club motto, Royal Troon Golf Course, Troon, Ayrshire, Scotland

Keep on hitting it straight until the wee ball goes in the hole.
James Braid, British professional, c. 1910

What is Love compared with holing out before your opponent?
P. G. Wodehouse
"Archibald's Benefit," 1919

It is nothing new or original to say that golf is played one stroke at a time. But it took me many years to realize it.

> **Bobby Jones**
> *Down the Fairway*, 1927

Me boy, never go to school on another man's club or ye'll not make a penny in this game.

> **Willie MacFarlane, British professional, advice to the youngster Sam Snead**

How well you play golf depends on how well you control that left hand of yours.

> **Tommy Armour**

The average expert player—if he is lucky—hits six, eight or ten real shots in a round. The rest are good misses.

> **Tommy Armour**

That little white ball won't move until you hit it, and there's nothing you can do after it has gone.

> **Babe Didrikson Zaharias**

People could make the world a nice place to live . . . if there weren't so goddamn many of them.

> **Clayton Heafner**

The Oldest Member: I always advise people never to give advice.

> **P. G. Wodehouse**
> "Tangled Hearts," 1948

Relax? How can anybody relax and play golf? You have to grip the club, don't you?

> **Ben Hogan**
> *Time*, 1949

I had gained an insurance stroke I hadn't deserved. Luck may be the residue of careful planning, as the wise men say, or it can be just plain luck.

Gene Sarazen
Thirty Years of Championship Golf, 1950

Nobody ever looked up and saw a good shot.

Don Herold
Love That Golf, 1952

You're only here for a short visit. Don't hurry, don't worry. And be sure to smell the flowers along the way.

Walter Hagen
The Walter Hagen Story, 1957

Put your ass into the ball, Mr. President.

Sam Snead, playing with Dwight D. Eisenhower

Lay off for three weeks and then quit for good.

Sam Snead, his advice to a pupil

Friends are a man's priceless treasures, and life rich in friendship is full indeed.

Bobby Jones, 1958

Always throw clubs ahead of you. That way you don't have to waste energy going back to pick them up.

Tommy Bolt, 1960

The eyes, during this time, are focused on a spot approximately 1/10 of an inch behind the ball and at a point on it that would correspond to the Tropic of Capricorn, if the ball can be imagined as a globe whose axis slants 23.5 degrees from the vertical away from the line of flight.

Rex Lardner
Out of the Bunker and Into the Trees, 1960

It's all right to put all your eggs in one basket—if you've got the right basket.

Sam Snead

If you sit and listen to the grass grow, sometimes your mind opens to ideas you've been missing.

Sam Snead, on taking time off from golf
The Education of a Golfer, 1962

One thing that's always available on a golf course is advice. If you play like I do, you think everybody knows something you don't know. If I see a bird fly over, I think he's going to tell me something.

Buddy Hackett
The Truth About Golf and Other Lies, 1968

A cardinal rule for the club breaker is never to break your putter and driver in the same match or you are dead.

Tommy Bolt
How to Keep Your Temper on the Golf Course, 1969

The slow-play habit, let me say, is like the cigarette habit—it is so hard to break that a man is wisest not to begin it.

Jack Nicklaus
The Greatest Game of All, 1969

I'd like to know where in heck half of my tax dollar goes. If I were president of a small country, I think I'd start a war against my neighbor, so the United States or Russia would jump in and give me a million dollars. Then the other one would give my neighbor a million. It's darn foolish.

Ben Hogan
Golf Digest, 1970

You have to know where you'll wind up before you start—
otherwise you'll go broke.

Ben Hogan
Golf Digest, 1970

If you think you can, or if you think you can't—you're right.
Deane Beman, his motto
Golf Digest, 1973

Serenity is knowing that your worst shot is still going to be
pretty good.

Johnny Miller
Sports Illustrated, 1975

Studying psychology isn't that relevant to the tour. . . . What
college really prepares you for is graduate school.

Tom Watson
Golf Digest, 1977

Don't let the bad shots get to you. Don't let yourself become
angry. The true scramblers are thick-skinned. And they always
beat the whiners.

Paul Runyan
Golf Digest, 1977

Golf is not a game you can rush. For every stroke you try to
force out of her, she is going to extract two strokes in return.
Dave Hill
Teed Off, 1977

Never do anything stupid.

Ben Crenshaw, his philosophy
Texas Monthly, 1977

Have a blast while you last.

> **Hollis Stacy, message on her T-shirt**
> *Golf Digest,* 1977

My goal is to play seventy-two holes someday without changing expression.

> **Jack Renner**
> *Sports Illustrated,* 1979

Never give up. If we give up in this game, we'll give up on life. If you give up that first time, it's easier to give up the second, third, and fourth times.

> **Tom Watson**
> *Golf Digest,* 1979

If the following foursome is pressing you, wave them through and then speed up.

> **Deane Beman, PGA Tour Commissioner**

The golfer who stands at the ball as rigid as a statue usually becomes a monumental failure.

> **Dick Aultman**
> *Golf Digest,* 1981

Golf is a friend. A friend is an antidote for despair.

> **Bob Toski**
> *Golf Digest,* 1981

He never backed off from anything, and I like that. No way would he ever have been penalized for slow play. He'd just step up and knock the hell out of the ball.

> **Lee Trevino, on Harry S Truman**
> *They Call Me Super Mex,* 1982

There are two things that won't last long in this world, and that's dogs chasing cars and pros putting for pars.

Lee Trevino
PGA Tour News, 1983

If you try to break the ball to pieces, the sod may fly farther than your shots. You've got to be gentle. Sweet-talk that ball. Make it your friend and it will stay with you a lot longer.

Sam Snead
Golf Digest, 1983

There are three types of bad shots in golf: those that cost you a half stroke, those that cost you a full stroke and those that cost you two strokes. Only stupidity costs you more than two strokes.

Bob Toski
Golf Digest, 1983

There ain't no point in loafing with a broke because nothing falls off.

George Low, on associating with rich people
The Master of Putting, 1983

I'll be the better for this tournament. After all, a smooth sea never produced a skillful sailor.

Mac O'Grady, after a closing-round eighty at the Bing Crosby National Pro-Am
Sports Illustrated, 1984

I just wish all the people in the world could get together and stop this fussin' and fightin'. What a hell of a world it would be.

Sam Snead
San Francisco Chronicle, 1984

Son, those clubs don't know you won The Masters. You'd better get after it.

> **Jackie Burke, advice to Ben Crenshaw**
> *Seattle Post-Intelligencer,* 1984

I try to have peace of mind. If you have that, you are a mental millionaire. It doesn't cost anything.

> **Chi Chi Rodriguez**
> *Seattle Post-Intelligencer,* 1984

There are two great rules of life—never tell everything at once.

> **Ken Venturi**
> "NEC World Series of Golf," CBS-TV, 1984

26. Practice and Lessons

Y'know it's hard to teach the game. Man's like a narrow-mouthed whiskey bottle. He can only take a word or two at a gulp. Ye have to take it slow.

> **Alec (Nipper) Campbell, Scottish teaching pro**
> *The American Golfer,* 1933

What a shame to waste those great shots on the practice tee. . . . I'd be afraid to stand out there and work at my game like that. I'd be afraid of finding out what I was doing wrong.

> **Walter Hagen**

Six years are needed to make a golfer—three years to learn the game, then another three to unlearn all you have learned in the first three years. You *might* be a golfer when you arrive at this stage, but more likely you're just starting.

Walter Hagen

If I miss one day's practice I know it; if I miss two days the spectators know it, and if I miss three days the world knows it.

Ben Hogan, paraphrasing pianist Ignace Paderewski

If you can't outplay them, outwork them.

Ben Hogan

My game is impossible to help. Ben Hogan said every time he gave me a lesson it added two shots to his game.

Phil Harris, comedian

There are two things in life which Ben Hogan especially dislikes. One is losing a golf match. The other is teaching golf.

Jimmy Demaret
My Partner, Ben Hogan, 1954

Your first lesson is over. Ben Hogan can rest easy.

Jimmy Demaret, to writer Milton Gross

Hell, this is only Wednesday. Nobody ever made any money on Wednesday.

Jimmy Demaret, practicing badly

You've just one problem. You stand too close to the ball—after you've hit it.

Sam Snead, to a pupil

Can anyone name the "greatest" atomic energy scientist? Yet, designing, engineering and constructing an atomic bomb is simple compared to trying to teach a fellow how to stop shanking.

Tommy Armour
Golfing, 1952

You have to build up the pupil's belief that you are delighted to see that the pupil isn't as hopelessly bad as he thinks he is.

Billy Burke
Golfing, 1952

You make twenty mistakes going into your backswing and correct ten of them coming forward, but unfortunately you haven't quite balanced your budget.

Harry Obitz, teaching pro, to a student

The best time to visit the driving range is at night when you can hardly see the ball.

Stephen Baker
How to Play Golf in the Low 120's, 1962

You can watch a champion hen lay eggs, but no matter how closely you observe the hen's form you will never be able to lay a real good egg.

Fred Beck
89 Years in a Sand Trap, 1965

The nice thing about these [golf] books is that they usually cancel each other out. One book tells you to keep your eye on the ball; the next says not to bother. Personally, in the crowd I play with, a better idea is to keep your eye on your partner.

Jim Murray
The Sporting World of Jim Murray, 1968

What did you expect from the U.S. Open champion—ground balls?

Lee Trevino, to an admiring spectator on the practice tee, 1969

Golf Pro: An optimistic doctor who has a cure for dying.

Jim Bishop, syndicated column, 1970

I don't need practice. I need a miracle.

Bruce Ashworth, after an eighty-two at the U.S. Open, 1973

If you're not prepared, somewhere in the quiz there are going to be some questions you can't answer.

Charles Coody, on the need for practice, 1974

Golf got complicated when I had to wear shoes and begin thinking about what I was doing.

Sam Snead

Watching Sam Snead practice hitting golf balls is like watching a fish practice swimming.

John Schlee
Golf Digest, 1977

Gary [Player] solicits far too much advice on the practice tee—I've seen him taking a lesson at the U.S. Open from a hot dog vendor.

Dave Hill
Teed Off, 1977

The harder you work, the luckier you get.

Gary Player

Not a week goes by without my learning something new about golf. That means, of course, that I was ignorant of eight things about golf two months ago. Extend that process back nearly twenty years and the result is an impressive accumulation of ignorance.

Peter Dobereiner
The World of Golf, 1981

Well, at $9.95 it did me some good.

Big Cat Williams, when told by a reader that his instruction book didn't do him any good, 1981

Try chipping to a tape of either REO Speedwagon or Huey Lewis and the News. It does wonders for your game.

Juli Inkster, practicing with a Sony Walkman
Sports Illustrated, 1982

I am the most over-taught and under-learned golfer in the U.S.A.

Herb Graffis, golf writer and editor
PGA Magazine, 1983

I just had a sixty-four. Boy, that's some shootin', isn't it? But Monday and Tuesday practice golf out here is like a boxer working on the punching bag. It doesn't hit back.

Chi Chi Rodriguez
New York Times, 1984

More instruction material on how to hit a middle iron is written in America during any six-month period than has been written about thoracic surgery since doctors stopped working out of the back rooms of barbershops.

Peter Andrews
Golf Digest, 1984

27. Pressure

I am so tense at times like that, I can hear the bees farting.
Mick O'Louglin, Irish pro, after a tough match, 1938

One always feels that he is running from something without knowing what nor where it is.
Bobby Jones, on tournament pressure

Everybody has two swings: the one he uses during the last three holes of a tournament and the one he uses the rest of the time.
Toney Penna, American professional

Doctors and mind experts go around explaining that it's perfectly okay to explode on the course because it releases your built-up tensions. They don't tell you, though, how you can rave like a wild beast and break ninety.
Sam Snead
The Education of a Golfer, 1962

It's that you lose *nerves,* not nerve. You can shoot lions in the dark and yet you can quiver like a leaf and fall flat over a two-foot putt.
Johnny Farrell, American professional

Sometimes a particular hole will cause a choke—a choke hole. Like the eighteenth at Cypress. It's like walking into a certain room in a big dark house when you were a kid—you get this fear that hits you.
Dave Marr

153

I was trying to get so far ahead I could choke and still win.

Lee Trevino, at the U.S. Open, which he won by four strokes over Jack Nicklaus, 1968

If this was any other tournament but The Masters, I'd have shot sixty-six. But I was choking out there. That green coat plays castanets with your knees.

Chi Chi Rodriguez, following a round of seventy, 1970

Every day, every minute, the greens get a little more difficult to read, and the fairways grow narrower.

Frank Beard, on The Masters' pressure, 1970

Q: Are you nervous?
Mann: No, I'm not, but my golf ball must be.

Carol Mann, as her ball blew off the tee
Golf Digest, 1970

Pressure is something every golfer feels at one time or another. . . . Sometimes when I putted I looked like a monkey trying to wrestle a football.

Sam Snead
Golf Digest, 1970

You don't know what pressure is until you play for five bucks with only two in your pocket.

Lee Trevino
Newsweek, 1971

When we come down to the final holes, some people find it very . . . hard . . . to breathe.

Jack Nicklaus, 1975

Anyone who hasn't been nervous, or who hasn't choked some-where down the line, is an idiot.

Dr. Cary Middlecoff
Golf Digest, 1977

More so than the fans think, it's a game of who chokes the least.

Dave Hill
Teed Off, 1977

The person I fear most in the last two rounds is myself.
Tom Watson, at the U.S. Open, 1977

A lot of guys who have never choked, have never been in the position to do so.

Tom Watson
Seattle Post-Intelligencer, 1978

It's awfully hard to smile when you're choking to death.
Gary Player, on the last round of his fourth Masters' victory
Minneapolis Tribune, 1978

Everyone has his own choking level, a level at which he fails to play his normal golf. As you get more experienced, your choking level rises.

Johnny Miller
Golf Digest, 1979

We all choke, and the man who says he doesn't choke is lying like hell. We all leak oil.

Lee Trevino
Golf World, 1980

Pressure is going out there on the golf course and thinking, "If I don't do well, I'll have to rob another bank."

> **Rick Meissner, former touring pro and convicted bank robber**
> *Esquire,* 1980

There's not as much pressure on the golf tour. Walking to the first tee is in no way comparable to walking through the jungle in combat.

> **Larry Nelson, former Vietnam infantry leader**
> *Golf Digest,* 1980

I don't think I had enough sense to know what pressure was.

> **Gene Sarazen, on playing Walter Hagen**
> *The New Yorker,* 1982

Class, someone once said, is the ability to undergo pressure with grace. So what did I do? I just did what comes naturally. I vomited.

> **Charles Price, on leading the 1964 British Open**
> *Golfer-At-Large,* 1982

Man, I couldn't even breathe. I couldn't smile because my lips were stuck to my teeth.

> **JoAnne Carner, on the win which put her into the LPGA Hall of Fame**
> *San Francisco Chronicle,* 1982

I used to think pressure was standing over a four-foot putt knowing I had to make it. I learned that real pressure was sixty-five people waiting for their food with only thirty minutes left on their lunch-hour break.

> **Amy Alcott, on waitressing in the off-season**
> *The Sporting News,* 1983

I had a three-foot putt for $30,000. I made the putt, but my knuckles were white, and do you know how hard I have to squeeze the putter to get my knuckles white?

Lee Trevino

"Bob Hope Desert Classic," NBC-TV, 1983

To what degree are you able to absorb the anxiety and pressure of this thing called the PGA Tour? . . . They have pills that can save you from absorbing radioactive isotopes. Perhaps they can develop a pill to protect us from the radioactivity of the tour.

Mac O'Grady

Sports Illustrated, 1984

I'd like to thank all my parents.

Juli Inkster, at the victory presentation

"Nabisco Dinah Shore Invitational," NBC-TV, 1984

There's no pressure. Mediocrity knows no pressure.

Gary McCord

Golf Digest, 1984

28. Putting

A man who can approach does not require to putt.

J. H .Taylor, British professional

Those who cannot drive suppose themselves to be good putters.

Sir Walter Simpson

The Art of Golf, 1887

This putting is wicked. It is sinful.
>   **James Braid, at the British Open, 1900**

Miss 'em quick!
>   **Macdonald Smith, American tournament professional**

Putting is not golf but croquet.
>   **A. A. Milne**
>   *Not That It Matters,* 1919

Talking turkey to a businessman, you must look squarely at him during the entire conversation. It's the same with putting. When you're talking turkey on the green, the face of your putter must look squarely at the hole.
>   **Gene Sarazen**

Suffering _____! I've got a hen back home in Charlotte that can lay an *egg* further than that!
>   **Clayton Heafner, upon missing a three-inch putt to**
>   **give Jimmy Demaret the Oakland Open by one stroke**

Drown, you sonofabitch. You'll never three-putt on me again!
>   **Ky Laffoon, dousing his putter after three-putting**
>   **two straight greens**

Golf is really two games. One is the game in the air. The golfer can lick that part of the game.
>   **Claude Harmon**

Reading a green is like reading the small type in a contract. If you don't read it with painstaking care, you are likely to be in trouble.
>   **Claude Harmon**

I am still undecided as to which of these two is the hardest shot in golf for me—any unconceded putt, or the explosion shot off the first tee. Both have caused me more strokes than I care to write about.

Ring Lardner, American writer

Even when times were good, I realized that my earning power as a golf professional depended on too many ifs and putts.

Gene Sarazen
Thirty Years of Championship Golf, 1950

The yips are that ghastly time when, with the first movement of the putter, the golfer blacks out, loses sight of the ball and hasn't the remotest idea of what to do with the putter or, occasionally, that he is holding a putter at all.

Tommy Armour

I had a long putt for an eleven.

Clayton Heafner, on why he took a twelve

A noted psychiatrist's wife asked him why he never let her play golf with him. "My dear," he admonished her, "there are three things a man must do alone: testify, die, and putt."

Bennett Cerf
The Laugh's on Me, 1959

If you couldn't putt you'd be selling hot dogs outside the ropes.

Billy Casper

Confidence builds with successive putts. The putter, then, is a club designed to hit the ball partway to the hole.

Rex Lardner
Out of the Bunker and Into the Trees, 1960

I putted like Joe Schmoe, and I'm not even sure Joe would appreciate that.

Arnold Palmer, at The Masters, 1960

That's a bagful of indecisions.

Jackie Burke, on Arnold Palmer's eight putters

Arnie, you're gonna have to buy a bigger jet just to carry all the putters.

Fuzzy Zoeller, as Palmer took six putters to the practice green

I'll tell you why putts go in. Because the old National Open champion in the sky puts 'em in.

Bob Rosburg, 1962

Hell, I'd putt sitting up in a coffin if I thought I could hole something.

Gardner Dickinson, on his putting styles, 1962

Everyone wants to be known as a great striker of the ball, for some reason. Nobody wants to be called a lucky, one-putting s.o.b., and nobody thinks he is.

Gary Player, 1962

I call my putter "Sweet Charity" because it covers such a multitude of sins from tee to green.

Billy Casper, 1963

I was on the dance floor, but I couldn't hear the band.

Chi Chi Rodriguez, on a fifty-foot putt

My putting was atrocious. I changed grips, stance, you name it. I tried everything but standing on my head.

Arnold Palmer, at the U.S. Open, 1968

Actually, I was always more of a breaker than a thrower—most of them putters. I broke so many of those, I probably became the world's foremost authority on how to putt without a putter.

Tommy Bolt
How to Keep Your Temper on the Golf Course, 1969

The devoted golfer is an anguished soul who has learned a lot about putting just as an avalanche victim has learned a lot about snow.

Dan Jenkins
The Dogged Victims of Inexorable Fate, 1970

Prayer never seems to work for me on the golf course. I think this has something to do with my being a terrible putter.

Rev. Billy Graham

The trouble with golf is you're only as good as your last putt.

**Doug Sanders, after missing a short putt on the
eighteenth to cost him the British Open
Championship, 1970**

The way I putted, I must've been reading the greens in Spanish and putting them in English.

**Homero Blancas, Mexican-American professional,
after an opening round eighty-one at The Masters, 1970**

When the hole is back here, I'm down there. When the hole is down there, I'm up here.

**Chi Chi Rodriguez, as he faced a sixty-foot putt at
The Masters, 1970**

But the bitter, inescapable truth remains. Once you've had 'em, you've got 'em.

> **Henry Longhurst, on the yips**
> *Golf Digest,* 1973

That sure is a small ball you're trying to swing at. And it sure is a long way to that green. And when you get there that cup is not exactly as big as a corporation president's ego.

> **Dan Jenkins**
> *Dead Solid Perfect,* 1974

Observer: Didn't you have any uphill putts?
Blancas: Sure. After each of my downhill putts.

> **Homero Blancas, after shooting a seventy-seven in the U.S. Open at Winged Foot, 1974**

Good luck on this putt. They've got the original president of this club buried right there.

> **Lee Trevino, as Dave Stockton faced a bumpy putt on the first green at the U.S. Open, 1974**

Putting is Clutch City. . . . Usually my putting touch deserts me under pressure. From five feet in to the hole you're in the throw-up zone.

> **Dave Hill**
> *Teed Off,* 1977

Putting from that distance [ninety feet] is a little like trying to touch a girl sitting on the far side of a couch. You can reach her, but you're not likely to accomplish much.

> **Charles Price**
> *Golf Magazine,* 1977

When our putting is sour, . . . then we are in honest, interminable, miserable trouble.

> **Arnold Palmer, c. 1970s**

I'm going to sleep with my putter tonight. My husband Don is going to have to sleep in the other bed.
> **JoAnne Carner, after a hot putting round in the Lady Keystone Open, 1980**

The divorce is from my old putter. I think it's final—at least we're due for a long separation. I've suffered with that old putter for two years now. It got so rude I couldn't stand it.
> **Shelley Hamlin**
> *Golf Digest,* 1980

That putt was so good I could feel the baby applauding.
> **Donna White, seven months pregnant, after sinking a long putt**
> *Sports Illustrated,* 1981

My mother always putts up on the toes of her left foot and whistling. Everyone thinks she is so cool and casual. But I know it's her way to beat the yips.
> **Al Geiberger**
> *Golf Magazine,* 1982

Putting isn't golf. Greens should be treated almost the same as water hazards: You land on them, then add two strokes to your score.
> **Chi Chi Rodriguez**
> *Golf Magazine,* 1983

I never really dreamed of making many putts. Maybe that's why I haven't made many.
> **Calvin Peete**
> *Sports Illustrated,* 1983

I've never once seen the cup move towards the ball.
> **Henry Longhurst, on a putt left short**
> "Nabisco Dinah Shore Invitational," NBC-TV, 1983

I think all that rain shrunk the cups.

> **Juli Inkster, after a poor putting day in the rain at the San Jose Classic, 1983**

I saw Sir Edmund Hillary out there, and he had to walk around the greens.

> **Tom Weiskopf, on the severely-sloped greens at the Tournament Players Club at Sawgrass**
> *USA Today*, 1983

That probably was the shortest putt I've ever missed when I was trying.

> **Hale Irwin, on a missed fifteen-inch putt at the Sea Pines Heritage Classic**
> *Golf Digest*, 1983

If God wanted you to putt cross-handed, he would have made your left arm longer.

> **Lee Trevino, on Tim Norris**
> "Bob Hope Classic," NBC-TV, 1984

Those are the kind, the six footers, that put a microphone in your hand.

> **Ken Venturi**
> "Bing Crosby National Pro-Am," CBS-TV, 1984

I've gotten rid of the yips four times, but they hang in there. You know those two-foot downhill putts with a break? I'd rather see a rattlesnake.

> **Sam Snead**
> *San Francisco Chronicle*, 1984

I don't have any big secret about putting. . . . Just hit at it. It's either going to miss or go in.

> **Ben Crenshaw**
> *San Francisco Chronicle*, 1984

He's got a putt that's almost out-of-town.
> **Lee Trevino, as Andy Bean faced an eighty-foot putt**
> "Honda Classic," NBC-TV, 1984

Let's take another look at that. You got a few minutes? It'll take that long for the ball to get to the hole.
> **Vin Scully, after Bean made his putt**
> "Honda Classic," NBC-TV, 1984

My caddie had the best answer for that—"Just to let the other one know it can be replaced."
> **Larry Nelson, on why he carried two putters**
> *Golf Digest,* 1984

Putts get real difficult the day they pass the money out.
> **Lee Trevino**
> "Isuzu-Andy Williams San Diego Open," NBC-TV, 1985

29. Real Golfers

They were real golfers, for real golf is a thing of the spirit, not of mere mechanical excellence of stroke.
> **P. G. Wodehouse**
> "A Woman Is Only a Woman," 1919

Real golfers, whatever the provocation, never strike a caddie with the driver. The sand wedge is far more effective.
> **Huxtable Pippey, San Francisco***

---

* The following quotations are taken from a Real Golfer contest held by Pat Sullivan for the *San Francisco Chronicle* in California.

Real golfers don't miss putts; they are "robbed."

John Thomas Trizuto, Hayward

Real golfers don't step on their opponent's ball while looking for it in the rough.

Jack Maloney, Vallejo

Real golfers always use a brand new ball on the sixteenth hole at Cypress Point.

Michael Gordon, San Francisco

Real golfers never eat quiche; they eat hot dogs and club sandwiches.

Jess Bragg, Carmel

Real golfers carry an eraser in case they get caught cheating.

Les Cochran, Guerneville

Real golfers don't use naked-lady tees.

Steve Lindroth, Truckee

Real golfers do not use their putters to get the ball out of the hole.

Dean F. James, PGA professional, Santa Rosa

Real golfers tape The Masters so they can go play themselves.

George W. Roope, Alameda

Real golfers never question their client's score.

D. G. Mix, Burlingame

Real golfers have two handicaps: one for braggin' and one for bettin'.

Bob Irons, Red Bluff

Real golfers always say: "It never rains on the golf course."
John Knapp, San Francisco

Real golfers go to work to relax.

George Dillon, San Ramon

Real golfers don't go in the bushes.

Bob Kunstel, Carmichael

Real golfers don't look at their caddies when they hand them a club.

Wesley R. Raines, Antioch

Real golfers don't cry when they line up their fourth putt.
Karen Hurwitz, Berkeley

Real golfers never complain about a hangover.

Bob Lane, Petaluma

Real golfers know how to count over five when they have a bad hole.

Dud Smith, San Francisco

Real golfers don't say, "Is that my friend in the trap or is the S.O.B. on the green?"

S. M. Leonard, Belmont

Real golfers don't stop to smell the flowers.

Walter E. Bearden, South San Francisco

Real golfers never pick up. This makes pro-ams a lot more fun to watch.

Golf Digest, 1983

Real golfers never take lessons. They give lessons—usually at cocktail parties.

Golf Digest, 1983

Real golfers never use metal woods. They own classic Tommy Armours, which accounts for the high incidence of poverty among real golfers.

Golf Digest, 1983

Real golfers don't care what real golfers do.

Lloyd N. Popish, Sunnyvale

30. Rules and Governing Bodies

There is only one way to play the game. You might as well praise a man for not robbing a bank.

Bobby Jones, on the 1925 U.S. Open when he penalized himself a stroke and lost the title by one shot

Players should pick up bomb and shell splinters from the fairways in order to save damage to the mowers.

War Rule, Britain, c. 1940s

If a ball comes to rest in dangerous proximity to a hippopotamus or crocodile, another ball may be dropped at a safe distance, no nearer the hole, without penalty.

Local Rule, Nyanza Club, British East Africa, c. 1950s

If a man is notified he has been appointed to serve on the rules committee for a certain tournament he should instantly remember that he must attend an important business meeting in Khartoum.

Herbert Warren Wind
Sports Illustrated, 1958

Golf, in fact, is the only game in the world in which a precise knowledge of the rules can earn one a reputation for bad sportsmanship.

Patrick Campbell
How to Become a Scratch Golfer, 1963

Next time? Next time, I bring my lawyer.

Robert de Vicenzo, on his 1968 disqualification from The Masters, 1970

Thou shalt not use profanity; thou shalt not covet thy neighbor's putter; thou shalt not steal thy neighbor's ball; thou shalt not bear false witness in the final tally.

Ground rules, clergyman's golf tournament, Grand Rapids, Michigan
Golf Magazine, 1974

You mustn't blow your nose when your partner is addressing the ball—otherwise the book of rules is mostly nonsense.

Henry Longhurst
The Best of Henry Longhurst, 1978

The entire handbook can be reduced to three rules. One: you do not touch your ball from the time you tee it up to the moment you pick it out of the hole. Two: don't bend over when you are in the rough. Three: when you are in the woods, keep clapping your hands.

Charles Price
Esquire, 1977

Golf is the hardest game in the world to play and the easiest to cheat at.

Dave Hill
Teed Off, 1977

There is no surer nor [more] painful way to learn a rule than to be penalized once for breaking it.

Tom Watson, author of a book on rules who was penalized two strokes
New York Times, 1980

The only times you touch the ball with your hand are when you tee it up and when you pick it out of the cup. The hell with television towers and cables and burrowing animals and the thousand and one things that are referred to as "not part of the golf course." If you hit the ball off the fairway, you play it from there.

Ken Venturi
Golf Magazine, 1981

Is it against the rule to carry a bulldozer in your bag?

Tom Watson, on the severe greens at the Tournament Players Club at Sawgrass
Sports Illustrated, 1982

I'd spend ninety-nine cents to make a buck.

George S. May, early golf promoter

He took the game away from the Scottish peasants and gave it to the American peasants.
Bob Harlow, *Golf World* publisher, on George S. May
Golf Magazine, 1981

The PGA? Well, that just goes to show you that no matter how closely you try to keep in touch with what's happening in Washington, the moment you turn your back the government has created another agency.
Lord Halifax, British ambassador to the United States, c. 1940s

Sir, would you mark yourself, please, while I try to get this one up?
Dave Marr, to a noisy gallery marshall, 1968

Perhaps, if A. W. Tillinghast had designed the Alamo, and the USGA had toughened it up, the Mexican siege would have failed.
Dick Schaap
Massacre at Winged Foot, 1974

The tour used to be run very nicely with five or six men on the field staff. Now we have eleven or twelve, so one guy can carry coffee over to the other.
Dave Hill
Teed Off, 1977

The PGA has had a number of officers whose IQs weren't much higher than their golf scores.
Charles Price
Golf Magazine, 1981

The USGA, whose sense of humor has always been on a par with that of the Internal Revenue Service.
Charles Price
Golf Magazine, 1981

When I retire, I'm going to get a pair of gray slacks, a white shirt, a striped tie, a blue blazer, a case of dandruff and go stand on the first tee so I can be a USGA official.

Lee Trevino
San Francisco Chronicle, 1981

We have the best officials in all sport—you don't see them until you need them.

Jerry Pate
Golf Magazine, 1982

Anybody who's played golf as long as I have and hit the ball as I do has got to be tough. You've got to be thick-skinned when you're looking at the green with a four-wood in your hand.

Deane Beman, PGA Tour Commissioner
Golf Digest, 1983

I know where all the holes are. Unlike the USGA, the R&A doesn't get some turkeys to go and change the holes around.

Lanny Wadkins, on why he wasn't practicing at
St. Andrews for the British Open
Golf Digest, 1984

31. Scoring

Bob, you can't always be playing well when it counts. You'll never win golf tournaments until you learn to score well when you're playing badly.

Jim Barnes, teaching professional, advice to a
young Bobby Jones, c. 1915

The income tax has made more liars out of the American people than golf has.

Will Rogers, humorist

Some lies are believable and some are not. The technique of lying and the timing of lies are at least as important as mastering the drive.

Rex Lardner
Out of the Bunker and Into the Trees, 1960

A pastime that has since created more lying Americans than any other save fishing.

Charles Price, on golf
The World of Golf, 1962

How strange are the lapses of human memory—and none more strange than those suffered by people who play, attempt to play, or watch the game of golf.

Henry Longhurst, golf writer, 1965

One of the troubles with a very high handicap is that the owner is either looked upon as a poor golfer or a possible cheat.

George Plimpton
The Bogey Man, 1968

You play the game by the rules and that in itself is an infallible mark of a gentleman of quality. Nobody ever cheats anybody else at golf. The one who is cheated is the one who cheats.

Tommy Armour
A Round of Golf with Tommy Armour, 1969

Gimme-A-Seven: The player's words to the scorekeeper after carding an eleven.

Jim Bishop, syndicated column, 1970

One good thing about shooting the way I've been shooting. You get to play early while the greens are still smooth.
Arnold Palmer, at The Masters, 1970

I'm playing like Tarzan—and scoring like Jane.
Chi Chi Rodriguez, at The Masters, 1970

"Shot a sixty-nine," he says, "but I played badly." Only Jack Nicklaus can play badly at Augusta and shoot a sixty-nine.
Dick Schaap
The Masters, 1970

Well, in plain old shitty English, I'm driving it bad, chipping bad, putting bad, and not scoring at all. Other than that, and the fact I got up this morning, I guess everything's okay.
Bob Wynn, 1975

One player high on the list of all-time money winners has cheated for years. . . . I always say he's advanced the ball farther illegally than Jimmy Brown has carried it for the Cleveland Browns.
Dave Hill
Teed Off, 1977

Golf is a game in which you yell Fore, shoot six, and write down five.
Paul Harvey, news commentator
Golf Digest, 1979

January: Man, how many do you want to win by, Sam?
Snead: You never know, them folks up ahead might be cheatin'.
Don January and Sam Snead, winning the Legends of Golf by twelve shots
Sports Illustrated, 1982

Golf appeals to the idiot in us and the child. What child does not grasp the pleasure-principle of miniature golf? Just how childlike golf players become is proven by their frequent inability to count past five.

John Updike
U.S. Amateur Championship program, 1982

The last time I birdied the first hole, I tried to lay up for the next seventeen.

Charles Price
Golfer-At-Large, 1982

I don't think that was me that shot that eighty-four. It must have been somebody else. Actually, I was trying to get my handicap squared away.

Fuzzy Zoeller, at the Greater Greensboro Open, 1982

It was ten years ago, and I've been down a lot of fairways since, and quite a bit of rough, too.

Johnny Miller, on his sixty-three at the U.S. Open
Golf Magazine, 1983

After that, I got myself together and bogeyed the last three.

Ben Crenshaw, on knocking three balls in the water
for an eleven at the fourteenth hole,
Sea Pines Heritage Classic, 1983

Golf is based on honesty. Where else would someone admit to a seven on an easy par three?

Jimmy Demaret

People who say golf is fun are probably the same people who rationalize the game by saying they play it for their health. What could be fun about a game in the entire history of which nobody has ever shot the score he thought he should have?

Charles Price
Golf Digest, 1983

It's good to be the first one in the clubhouse with a low score. You can't bogey from the scoreboard.

Lee Trevino
"Isuzu-Andy Williams San Diego Open," NBC-TV, 1984

I'm a nineteen and I think he's about a nineteen, but he cheats more than I do.

Dolores Hope, on her husband Bob's handicap
Golf Digest, 1983

It's hard to keep score like I do with someone looking over your shoulder.

Bob Hope
"Nabisco Dinah Shore Invitational," NBC-TV, 1983

32. Seniors

A game in which you claim the privileges of age, and retain the playthings of childhood.

Samuel Johnson, English literary figure, on golf

To that man, age brought only golf instead of wisdom.

George Bernard Shaw, British playwright

Golf, like measles, should be caught young, for, if postponed to riper years, the results may be serious.

P. G. Wodehouse
"A Mixed Threesome," 1920

Any game where a man sixty can beat a man thirty ain't no game.

Burt Shotten, major-league baseball manager

I can't stand the thought of shooting another eighty.

Walter Hagen, when asked why he was retiring, 1940s

My handicap? Arthritis.

Bobby Jones, age forty-five, 1947

It isn't golf, it's the traveling. I want to die an old man, not a young man.

Ben Hogan, cutting back on his schedule, 1949

Golf is like driving a car, as you get older you get more careful.

Sam Snead

Look at 'em! They roll 'em in from the middle of the fairway —no idea of how tough the game is. They'll learn, but the trouble is, there'll be a new crop of 'em along about this time next year. Just ain't no way of keeping ahead of 'em.

Sam Snead, on the youngsters on the tour, 1960s

Getting my first Social Security check.

Gene Sarazen, on his greatest thrill

I'm thirty-four, but a Puerto Rican thirty-four is like an American fifty.

Chi Chi Rodriguez, 1970

The fairways get longer and the holes get smaller.

Bobby Locke, age fifty-seven
Golf Digest, **1972**

People tell me just to put the putter down and putt, but that's like telling a guy to go stand still by a rattlesnake—easier said than done.

Sam Snead, age sixty-two
San Francisco Chronicle, 1974

A caddie watched him miss a short putt that second day at the Hope. "Hole used to be scared of him. He'd look at it and the hole got scared. Now he's scared of the hole. The hole knows it too."

Dan Gleason, on Arnold Palmer, at age forty-five
The Great, The Grand and the Also-Ran, 1976

When you're my age, you can't remember a practice round the next day, anyway.

Gene Sarazen, age seventy-four
Golf Digest, 1976

Sam Snead, trying to shoot his age the day after his sixty-fourth birthday, instead shot Cliff Roberts' age and missed the cut by two shots.

Bev Norwood, writing on Snead's eighty-three in the Memorial Tournament, 1976

Only old people follow me around now. Our eyesight isn't what it used to be. They can't see me and I can't see them.

Julius Boros, age fifty-seven, when asked if big crowds bothered him
Golf Digest, 1977

If I'm breathing heavy while walking on a green, I'm going uphill. If I trip, I'm going downhill.

David (Spec) Goldman, Dallas senior golfer, on how he reads greens
Golf Digest, 1979

My God, it looks like a wax museum!
> **George Low, former touring pro, at his first seniors'
> event, 1980**

Who does he think he is, Jack Nicklaus again?
> **Andy Bean, after Nicklaus won the PGA
> Championship at age forty, 1980**

I retired from competition at twenty-eight, the same age as Jones. The difference was that Jones retired because he beat everybody. I retired because I couldn't beat anybody.
> **Charles Price**
> *Golf Digest*, 1982

At twenty-five, I thought a course that wasn't seven thousand yards long was a joke. At fifty, I thought there ought to be a law against them.
> **Charles Price**
> *Golfer-At-Large*, 1982

If anybody yelled "sick call," the line would run all the way from the locker room to the first tee.
> **Doug Ford, on the Senior Tour**
> *Golf Magazine*, 1982

I have so many aches and pains that when I go outside my shadow refuses to come along.
> **Walter Burkemo, age sixty-four**
> *Golf Magazine*, 1982

What other sport holds out hope of improvement to a man or woman over fifty? . . . For a duffer like the above-signed, the room for improvement is so vast that three lifetimes could be spent roaming the fairways carving away at it, convinced that perfection lies just over the next rise.
> **John Updike**
> *U.S. Amateur Championship* program, 1982

When I was inducted into the World Golf Hall of Fame in September of 1981, I passed another milestone. Now I know that some day I can officially become a has-been.

Lee Trevino
They Call Me Super Mex, 1982

I can't tell if a putt is uphill or downhill, and all short putts look straight.

Sam Snead, age seventy
The Sporting News, 1983

The older you get, the longer you used to be.

Chi Chi Rodriguez
PGA Tour News, 1983

The Senior Tour is like a class reunion. It's the same as it was thirty years ago. We tell the same dirty jokes—only they're funnier now.

Bob Toski
Golf Digest, 1983

Like a lot of fellows around here, I have a furniture problem. My chest has fallen into my drawers.

Billy Casper, on the Senior Tour
The Sporting News, 1983

I really haven't given it much thought. After all, I won't become eligible for another 42 months, 5 days, 8½ hours.

Butch Baird, asked if he'd join the Senior Tour
Golf Digest, 1983

I'm like a '67 Cadillac. I've changed the engine twice, rolled back the odometer and replaced the transmission. But now all the tires are goin' flat. It's time to put it in the junkyard.

Lee Trevino, age forty-three
Washington Post, 1983

I don't have some long-range goal that I've always wanted to do after I grew up. What am I supposed to say? Yeah, I'm forty-three, and when I'm through with golf I'd like to be an astronaut?

Lee Trevino
Golf Digest, 1983

It kept me from taking an honest job. My theory is never work for a living if you don't have to.

Don January, on the Senior Tour
San Francisco Examiner, 1984

I don't mind getting old. There's a lot of people who won't allow it.

Phil Harris, age seventy-nine
"Bing Crosby National Pro-Am," CBS-TV, 1984

I never thought I'd live to shoot my age. I thought somebody would shoot me first.

Dale Morey, shooting a sixty-five on his sixty-fifth birthday
Golf Digest, 1984

My trouble is I can't turn. When you can't turn, you look at your driver after you hit it 'cause you think you left the head-cover on.

Sam Snead, age seventy-one
Golf Digest, 1984

This makes seven halls of fame I'm in. The one in West Virginia you have to either die or retire to get in, but the boys there said, "It don't look like he's gonna do either, so we better take down the bars and let him in."

Sam Snead
San Francisco Chronicle, 1984

I had forgotten just how sweet the click of a ball sounds.
Arnold Palmer, age fifty-four, on his new hearing aid
San Francisco Examiner, 1984

He's the king of kings. . . . There's a strength about the man that people want to be around. Anybody who resents Arnold getting more attention than the rest of us doesn't deserve to use his head for more than a hat rack.
Doug Sanders, on Arnold Palmer's popularity on the Senior Tour
Sports Illustrated, 1984

I didn't realize how long some of these seniors have been around. Yesterday I saw a guy signing his scorecard with a feather.
Bob Hope
Confessions of a Hooker, 1985

33. The Swing

There is one essential only in the golf swing, the ball must be hit.
Sir Walter Simpson
The Art of Golf, 1887

Golfers find it a very trying matter to turn at the waist, more particularly if they have a lot of waist to turn.
Harry Vardon

Those who think in terms of golf being a science unfortunately have tried to separate from each other the arms, head, shoulders, body, hips and legs. They turn the golfer into a worm that's been cut into bits, with each part wriggling every which way.

Ernest Jones, British teaching professional

Golf is an awkward set of bodily contortions designed to produce a graceful result.

Tommy Armour

Nobody ever swung the golf club too slowly.

Bobby Jones

He took a swing like a man with a wasp under his shirt and his pants on fire, trying to impale a butterfly on the end of a scythe.

Paul Gallico
Golf Is a Nice Friendly Game, 1942

Take it easily and lazily, because the golf ball isn't going to run away from you while you're swinging.

Sam Snead
How to Play Golf, 1946

Yes, you're probably right about the left hand, but the fact is that I take the checks with my right hand.

Bobby Locke, South African pro, on his weak left-hand grip, 1947

I once played with Henry Ford II and told him, "You can buy a country, but you can't buy a golf swing. It's not on a shelf."

Gene Sarazen

Ben Hogan would rather have a coral snake rolling inside his shirt than hit a hook.

Claude Harmon

Don't change the arc of your swing unless you are fairly sure you blundered in some way earlier.
Rex Lardner
Out of the Bunker and Into the Trees, 1960

The best place to refine your swing is, of course, right out on the practice range. . . . You will have an opportunity to make the same mistakes over and over again so that you no longer have to think about them, and they become part of your game.
Stephen Baker
How to Play Golf in the Low 120's, 1962

Hope: What do you think of my swing?
Palmer: I've seen better swings in a condemned playground.
Bob Hope and Arnold Palmer
"Chrysler Presents a Bob Hope Special," NBC-TV, 1963

Always fade the ball. You can't talk to a hook.

Dave Marr, 1968

Too many golfers grip the club at address like they were trying to choke a prairie coyote to death.
Curt Wilson, Las Vegas trick-shot artist
Golf Digest, 1970

Hook: The addiction of fifty percent of all golfers.
Slice: The weakness of the other half.
Jim Bishop, syndicated column, 1970

To get an elementary grasp of the game of golf, a human must learn, by endless practice, a continuous and subtle series of highly unnatural movements, involving about sixty-four muscles, that result in a seemingly "natural" swing, taking all of two seconds to begin and end.

Alistair Cooke, British journalist

How do I address the ball? I say, "Hello there, ball. Are you going to go in the hole or not?"

Flip Wilson
"The Flip Wilson Show," NBC-TV, 1972

Everybody has two swings—a beautiful practice swing and the choked-up one with which they hit the ball. So it wouldn't do either of us a damned bit of good to look at your practice swing.

Ed Furgol
Golf Magazine, 1974

Here we are, making thousands of dollars a year, and we're trying to change our swings.

Johnny Miller, on the practice tee
Golf Digest, 1974

The golf swing is like sex in this respect. You can't be thinking about the mechanics of the act while you're performing.

Dave Hill
Teed Off, 1977

"We know a lot about the swing," one college golf coach said to me, "but not much about how to help golfers learn it."

W. Timothy Gallwey
The Inner Game of Golf, 1979

I remember being upset once and telling my Dad I wasn't following through right, and he replied, "Nancy, it doesn't make any difference to a ball what you do after you hit it."

Nancy Lopez
The Education of a Woman Golfer, 1979

The only thing that you should force in a golf swing is the club back into the bag.

Byron Nelson

We are getting too mechanical about the golf swing. . . . Golf was never meant to be an exact science—it's an art form. Einstein was a great scientist but a lousy golfer.

Bob Toski
Golf Digest, 1981

Just hit the ball and go chase it. You will probably make your best effort on each shot.

Johnny Miller
Golf Magazine, 1982

If a great swing put you high on the money list, there'd be some of us who would be broke!

Raymond Floyd
Golf Magazine, 1982

Golferswhotalkfastswingfast.

Bob Toski
Golf Digest, 1982

No one who ever had lessons would have a swing like mine.
Lee Trevino
"The Tonight Show," NBC-TV, 1983

I still swing the way I used to, but when I look up the ball is going in a different direction.

> **Lee Trevino**
> *Golf Digest*, 1984

You show me a player who swings out of his shoes and I'll show you a player who isn't going to win enough to keep himself in a decent pair of shoes for very long.

> **Sam Snead**
> *Golf Digest*, 1984

If that ball hit the 17-Mile-Drive, it'll be a 23-mile-drive.

> **Vern Lundquist, on a slice at Pebble Beach**
> "Bing Crosby National Pro-Am," CBS-TV, 1984

I've been squeezing the club so hard the cow is screaming.

> **J.C. Snead**
> "Honda Classic," NBC-TV, 1984

34. Tournaments

Look at that little pissy-assed medal of yours. I got real dough.

> **Jock Hutchison, to amateur Chick Evans at the U.S. Open, 1916**

I've seen more people on the back of a motorcycle.

> **George Low, to Bing Crosby, on the crowds at his fledgling tournament, c. 1940s**

Hell, I didn't even know he was in the field. I thought he was there peddling headcovers or something.

> **Sam Snead, on Toney Penna, who defeated him in the North-South Open, 1948**

I wouldn't send my mother-in-law out to plow in weather like this.

> **Dave Smith, on the fog at the U.S. Amateur in Broadmoor, Colorado, 1959**

I hope I don't upset Jack's game. No one has ever watched me play but cows.

> **Hans Schweizer, Swiss golfer, on being paired with Jack Nicklaus at the World Team Amateur Championship, 1960**

Now on the pot, Johnny Tee.

> **Announcer on first tee of the Los Angeles Open, introducing Johnny Pott, c. 1960s**

The record book has me down for a seventy-nine on the final day. That looks pretty woeful, but considering what happened the night before it was a pretty good round of golf.

> **Tony Lema, on the 1959 San Diego Open**
> *Golfer's Gold,* 1964

Reporter: What happened, Marty?
Fleckman: I got back on my game. That's all.

> **Marty Fleckman, on shooting an eighty after leading after three rounds of the U.S. Open, 1967**

When they say they have a "Sudden Death Play-Off," it's not always just a figure of speech. You need penicillin in your bag more than a one-iron. It's known to some of the pros as "The VapoRub Open."

> **Jim Murray, on the Bing Crosby National Pro-Am**
> *The Sporting World of Jim Murray,* 1968

My wife's got a broken wrist, we've got a ten-week-old baby, and our dog's pregnant. I came out here to rest.
Lee Trevino, at the Byron Nelson Classic, 1969

These greens are so bad the Dallas Cowboys wouldn't play on 'em. They ought to plow 'em up and plant 'em with potatoes.
Lee Trevino, at the World Cup in Buenos Aires, 1970

My putter had a heart attack the last nine holes and just died on me.
Lanny Wadkins, after leading for three rounds and slipping to fourth in the Byron Nelson Classic, 1973

I'd played in the Open before, of course. Several times. And I'd been in all of the other majors now and then. But I'd never been any closer to the lead than the parking lot.
Dan Jenkins
Dead Solid Perfect, 1974

The greens are the biggest joke since Watergate.
Lee Trevino, on the Victorian Open played at Royal Lemborne, Melbourne, Australia, 1974

The fourteenth hole was the turning point. When I four-putted for the second time, I knew I was in trouble.
Bill Erfurth, Chicago club pro, on shooting an eighty-eight at the U.S. Open at Winged Foot, 1974

I'd take a bottle of Nytol, wash it down with a bottle of Nyquil, and then I'd think about falling asleep.
Tom Jenkins, leader after the third round of the U.S. Open, when asked how he'd spend his evening, 1974

They used to play the Robinson Fall Classic in Robinson, Illinois. Errol Flynn could not get laid in Robinson, Illinois, with a two-million-dollar bill.

John Jacobs, 1975

The pin placements weren't too tough, but whoever set them missed ten greens.

Leonard Thompson, at the Greater Greensboro Open, 1975

Trying to catch Nicklaus from that far back is like trying to climb Mt. Everest in street shoes.

Tom Kite, eight shots behind after two rounds of the Sea Pines Heritage Classic, 1975

There was a sign near the entrance to I-80 that read: Welcome to Bettendorf, Iowa's Most Exciting City. They decided that that sign must've been put up there by the state to avoid overpopulation.

Dan Gleason, on the Quad Cities Open
The Great, The Grand and the Also-Ran, **1976**

You wait till the last two days, when the teams who are out of it start getting drunk and screwing off while you're trying to win the tournament. That's when it's a zoo.

Dave Hill, on the Bing Crosby National Pro-Am, 1976

Man, the day them Canadian bankers cash a check for a Mexican is the same day you gonna boogie with Lester Maddox's daughter.

Lee Trevino, to his caddie Herman Mitchell, at the Canadian Open, 1978

The only way I could have beaten him was if he fell into a lake and couldn't swim.

George Bayer, on losing to Don January by eight shots in the PGA Senior's Championship, 1980

It wasn't much fun being an amateur. I got tired of polishing the silverware.
>**Patty Sheehan**
>*San Jose Mercury News,* 1980

It was a very long day. I don't know how long we've been out here, but I know it's time to shave again.
>**Fuzzy Zoeller, on playing thirty-six holes on the final day of the rain-delayed Colonial National Invitation tournament, 1981**

Some girl in sprayed-on jeans followed him around all day, which just proves that even Nathaniel can be distracted.
>**Kathryn Crosby, as her son Nathaniel shot an eighty in qualifying for the U.S. Amateur, 1981**

Everybody in my family is talented. My father, my mother, my brother, my sister Mary. She shot J. R. Gosh, I had to win the Amateur.
>**Nathaniel Crosby, on winning the U.S. Amateur, 1981**

I hadn't won in so long, I wanted to be sure this one soaked in.
>**Jerry Pate, after he jumped in the lake upon winning the Danny Thomas–Memphis Classic, 1982**

The ball jumped out of the hole and hit me on the foot. Technically, it was only a seven-putt green.
>**Jerry Pate, after taking nine shots from the fringe at Firestone's second hole at the World Series of Golf, 1982**

I shot a Red Grange today—seventy-seven. Somebody should have shot me. I looked like I needed a white cane.
>**Tom Watson, at the U.S. Open, 1982**

It looked like a civil rights march out there. People were afraid we were going to steal their hubcaps.

Chi Chi Rodriguez, on being paired with Homero Blancas and Rod Curl at the Anderson–Pacific Golf Classic, 1983

Hell, he's been one back, or one or two ahead, all his life.

Jay Haas, leading the Los Angeles Open, asked if he was worried about Jack Nicklaus, one shot back, 1984

This is a nice tournament. Of course, you have to caddie for Bob Hope before you get an invitation.

Joey Bishop, comic
"Bob Hope Classic," NBC-TV, 1984

At our first tournament, the groundskeeper was a lizard.

Bob Hope, on the Bob Hope Classic
USA Today, 1984

I realize that's why we play golf, to hit the ball into the hole. But it's such a strange feeling when you hit a shot and it actually goes in.

Hollis Stacy, after holing a 123-yard 7-iron at the U.S. Women's Open, 1984

They ought to give away the car for hitting the green at all.

Mark McCumber, on the car given away for an ace at the windblown seventh hole at the Honda Classic, 1984

You have no defense for their offense.

Curtis Strange, trying to catch leader Willie Wood
"Kingsmill Classic," NBC-TV, 1984

From April to August, I went to so many golf tournaments I felt like an alligator on a shirt pocket.

Dan Jenkins
Life Its Ownself, 1984

I got a room once for $36 a night. At Pebble Beach, that was my major accomplishment.

Gary McCord, on the Bing Crosby National Pro-Am, 1984

What do I think of the pin placements? I think every green should have a pin placement.

Gary McCord, at the Hawaiian Open, 1985

Fred Couples is having problems. He may tie that putter onto the back of his car and drag it all the way to the next tournament.

Lee Trevino
"Honda Classic," NBC-TV, 1985

35. Tour Players: Men

George Archer, American, born 1939

His personal life will never hurt his nerves. George's idea of a big night out is a hamburger at McDonald's and a science fiction movie.

Dave Hill
Teed Off, 1977

Tommy Armour, American, 1895–1968

He is as temperamental as a soprano with a frog in her throat.
Clarence Budington Kelland
The American Golfer, 1935

Seve Ballesteros, Spanish, born 1957

He goes after a golf course like a lion at a zebra. He doesn't reason with it; he tries to throw it out of the window or hold its head under water till it stops wriggling.
Jim Murray
Los Angeles Times, 1976

I'd like to see the fairways more narrow. Then everybody would have to play from the rough, not just me.
Seve Ballesteros, at the British Open
Golf Digest, 1979

Seve drives the ball into territory Daniel Boone couldn't find.
Fuzzy Zoeller, 1981

Seve's never in trouble. We see him in the trees quite a lot, but that looks normal to him.
Ben Crenshaw
Sports Illustrated, 1983

Trying to catch Seve is like a Chevy pickup trying to catch a Ferrari.
Tom Kite, at The Masters
The Sporting News, 1983

Sometimes I think the only way the Spanish people will recognize me is if I win the Grand Slam and then drop dead on the eighteenth green.
Seve Ballesteros, on his lack of recognition in his home country
Golf World, 1984

Miller Barber, American, born 1931

Miller has always been a bit of a hypochondriac. . . . His golf bag looks like something Marcus Welby might carry. . . . Before he heads for the first tee, "X" is armed and ready to face the wilderness.

> **Ben Crenshaw**
> *Golf Magazine,* 1981

When Barber swings, it looks as if his golf club gets caught in a clothesline.

> **Ben Crenshaw**
> *The Sporting News,* 1984

His swing reminds me a lot of a machine I once saw at a country fair making saltwater taffy. It goes in four directions and none of them seem right.

> **Buck Adams, director of golf, Country Club of North Carolina**
> *Golf World,* 1984

George Bayer, American, born 1925

If distance was a big factor, George Bayer should be retired now and matching gold pieces with those Greek shipowners on the Riviera.

> **Tommy Bolt**
> *How to Keep Your Temper on the Golf Course,* 1969

Andy Bean, American, born 1953

He's a superstar from the neck down.

> **David Ogrin**
> *Golf Digest,* 1984

Frank Beard, American, born 1939

He looks like a bad doctor from Elko, Nevada, whose chemistry set blew up and he's golfing for penance.

> **Don Rickles, comedian**

Tommy Bolt, American, born 1918

Tommy Bolt's putter has spent more time in the air than Lindbergh.

Jimmy Demaret

Turning off his temper is rather like capping Mount Vesuvius —interesting but impractical.

Jim Murray
Los Angeles Times

Julius Boros, American, born 1920

Julius Boros is all hands and wrists like a man dusting the furniture.

Tony Lema, on his swing
Golfer's Gold, 1964

He's Perry Como's kid by another marriage.

Don Rickles, comic

Gay Brewer, American, born 1932

Gay Brewer? I always thought he was a little fag wine maker from Modesto.

Phil Harris, to Chris Schenkel
"Bing Crosby National Pro-Am," ABC-TV, 1974

He swings the club in a figure eight. If you didn't know better, you'd swear he was trying to kill snakes.

Dave Hill
Teed Off, 1977

Rex Caldwell, American, born 1950

I have a reputation now of being an excellent putter. The other guys figure I must be putting good to win so much money, because the rest of my game is so bad.

Rex Caldwell
Golf Digest, 1978

"Rex has been a rabbit so long that his nose twitches when he gets around a salad bar," says one pro.

Barry McDermott
Sports Illustrated, 1983

I'm not your stereotyped golf pro. I say dirt when it's dirt.

Rex Caldwell
Sports Illustrated, 1983

Billy Casper, American, born 1931

Billy Casper, currently one of the best putters from four-hundred yards in to the hole that the tour has ever seen.

Tony Lema
Golfer's Gold, 1964

I feel sorry for Casper. He can't putt a lick. He missed three thirty-footers out there today.

Gary Player, at the U.S. Open, 1964

Billy could putt in a plowed field.

John Schlee
Golf Magazine, 1968

Allergic to everything but money and religion.

Mark Mulvoy and Art Spander
Golf: The Passion and the Challenge, 1977

Don Cherry, American, born 1924

Don has bark marks on his forehead from whacking his head against trees. He claims it's from hunting balls with his head down and running into trees, but those who know his temper know better.

Buddy Hackett
The Truth About Golf and Other Lies, 1968

Bobby Clampett, American, born 1960

He is a tall, slender young man who, from a distance, looks a bit like Harpo Marx in double knits.

Jim Moriarty
Sport, 1982

I told Bobby, "I don't like your golf swing and I never have." He had more moves than an erector set.

Jimmy Ballard, teaching professional
Golf Digest, 1984

Bobby Cole, South African, born 1948

Cole is the second shortest South African on the pro tour. . . . He is one inch taller than Gary Player and a million dollars poorer.

Dick Schaap
Massacre at Winged Foot, 1974

Charles Coody, American, born 1937

Charlie Coody is unbelievable. He'll give you his entire round right down to the number of tees he broke. When I see him, I say, "I hope you shot sixty-four, Charlie, so it'll take you only an hour to tell me about it."

Frank Beard
Golf Digest, 1975

Henry Cotton, British, born 1907

You couldn't tell whether Cotton was in the right or left side of the fairway because his ball was so close to the middle.

Bob Toski
Golf Digest, 1983

Bruce Crampton, Australian, born 1935

Bruce Crampton, an Australian who'd had a terrible time getting people to like him, even on those rare occasions when he tried.

Dan Gleason
The Great, The Grand and the Also-Ran, 1976

Ben Crenshaw, American, born 1952

He hits it in the woods so often he should get an orange hunting jacket.

Tom Weiskopf, 1979

I sometimes wonder if he shouldn't stop reading so much about golf history and start making some.

Dave Marr
Golf Digest, 1981

Ben is the best damn second-and-third-place finisher in the majors the world will ever know.

Kevin Cook
Playboy, 1982

I don't remember Ben ever missing a putt from the time he was twelve until he was twenty.

Tom Kite, after Crenshaw won The Masters, his first major
Sports Illustrated, 1984

Jimmy Demaret, American, 1910–1983

If Jimmy Demaret had won the money he would have been eight to five to leave it in a bar or blow it on a handmade pair of orange and purple saddle oxfords.

Dan Jenkins
The Dogged Victims of Inexorable Fate, 1970

Best Wind Player: This one easily goes to Jimmy Demaret. He could come in first in this category just using his mouth.

Charles Price
Golf Magazine, 1975

People say it was amazing that Jimmy could win three Masters almost without practicing. I think it's amazing he could win them almost without sleeping.

Sam Snead
Golf Digest, 1983

That's what caused both of my divorces, spending too much time with Jimmy.

Lee Trevino
"Legends of Golf," NBC-TV, 1984

Jim Dent, American, born 1939

Jim Dent is the longest hitter around today. He not only has a graphite shaft, he has graphite arms, too.

George Bayer
Golf Magazine, 1974

Roberto de Vicenzo, Argentinian, born 1923

Play good, Roberto, I'm betting on you to be low Mexican.

Jimmy Demaret

What player on the tour would you *least* want to figure your income tax?

**Dave Marr, referring to de Vicenzo's Masters'
scorecard incident, 1968**

Leo Diegel, American, 1899–1951

Leo Diegel, a perfectionist who unfortunately had the nerves of a schoolgirl.

Charles Price
The World of Golf, 1962

They keep trying to give me a championship, but I won't take it.

Leo Diegel

Lee Elder, American, born 1934

I like Lee. He's a cheerful, easygoing guy. He could sleep through the most important appointment of his life.

Dave Hill
Teed Off, 1977

Raymond Floyd, American, born 1942

Raymond has done it all. If he were playing Sunday in Miami and there was a party that night in Dallas, he'd charter a plane.

Lanny Wadkins
Golf Digest, 1982

Rod Funseth, American, born 1933

Funseth? He can't do it. Don't hit but one bucket of balls a year. Mother got in a sudden-death play-off there at Greensboro last year, and first thing he ask was how much second place worth.

Dan Gleason, quoting a caddie
The Great, The Grand and the Also-Ran, 1976

He attracted about as much attention as the PGA Tour's latest announcement that it was against slow play.

John P. May
Golf Digest, 1984

Ivan Gantz, American, born 1903

Worst temperament? . . . My choice has to be Ivan Gantz, who has long since abandoned the tour. He used to get so disgusted at himself that he threw clubs on the *practice tee!*

Charles Price
Golf Magazine, 1975

Al Geiberger, American, born 1937

There are certain things you don't believe in: the Easter Bunny, campaign promises, the Abominable Snowman, a husband with lipstick on his collar, and a guy who tells you he shot fifty-nine on his own ball—and his wife didn't keep score.

Jim Murray, on Geiberger's fifty-nine in the Danny Thomas Memphis Classic
Los Angeles Times, 1977

Hubert Green, American, born 1946

His swing looks like a drunk trying to find a keyhole in the dark.

Jim Murray
Los Angeles Times

I don't try to analyze my swing. I looked at it once on film and almost got sick.

Hubert Green
Golf Digest, 1977

He'll talk to a tree. . . . He'd be happy in a closet with a six-pack of beer.

Lee Trevino
They Call Me Super Mex, 1982

Aw, that's just Hubert over there fixing his golf swing.
Fuzzy Zoeller, hearing a chain saw
Golf Digest, 1983

Walter Hagen, American, 1892–1969

Walter is not a religious man. I know he believes in God, but if I ever wanted to go looking for him I wouldn't start with a church. I have an idea he's broken eleven of the Ten Commandments.
Fred Corcoran, executive director of the PGA, to Monsignor Robert Barry, 1940

Hagen could relax sitting on a hot stove. His touch was sensitive as a jeweller's scale. If he estimated a club's weight and the scales didn't check with Walter's guess, the scales were wrong.
Tommy Armour

One thing about Walter, he wouldn't spend your money any faster than he spends his own.
Bob Harlow, Hagen's manager

Golf has never had a showman like him. All the professionals who have a chance to go after the big money today should say a silent thanks to Walter each time they stretch a check between their fingers.
Gene Sarazen
Thirty Years of Championship Golf, 1950

He was not the pushy type and never sought an invitation. With the then Prince of Wales tagging Walter's footsteps, somehow he didn't have to.
Grantland Rice
The Tumult and the Shouting, 1954

He carried it off big. He was gorgeous. One got the impression that he had invented the game.

Charles Price
The World of Golf, 1962

Hagen spent money like a King Louis with a bottomless treasury. In the credit-card age, he might have broken American Express. As it was, he got by.

Al Barkow
Golf's Golden Grind, 1974

The best putters have almost invariably been slow movers. Walter Hagen took five minutes to reach for and lift a salt shaker, forty-five minutes to shave. He just *never* rushed into anything.

George Low
The Master of Putting, 1983

Chandler Harper, American, born 1914

Harper is a fellow who has been dogged with a lot of tough luck on the circuit (or so he tells you).

Jimmy Demaret
My Partner, Ben Hogan, 1954

Dutch Harrison, American, 1910–1982

If Dutch had thought as much about golf as he did about the track he would have been right there with Ben Hogan.

Tommy Bolt
The Hole Truth, 1971

Clayton Heafner, American, 1914–1960

Clayton Heafner. He's mad *all* the time.

> **Jimmy Demaret, asked which player on the tour had the most even disposition**

Clayton had a bad temper. The only time he could putt was when he was mad enough to *hate* the ball into the hole.

Dr. Cary Middlecoff
ESPN-TV, 1982

Lionel Hebert, American, born 1928

Here comes old Lionel Hebert. He'll either give you a lesson or take one.

Sam Snead

Dave Hill, American, born 1937

I had knee surgery late in 1973 and one of my smart-assed fellow pros said, "How's that going to help his head?"

Dave Hill
Teed Off, 1977

I'm crazy, but I have an advantage over most people. I know it.

Dave Hill
Teed Off, 1977

Ben Hogan, American, born 1912

It takes him three hours to go nine holes in practice. . . . He'll even memorize the grain of the grass. He'll putt 'til hell won't have it.

Clyde Starr, caddie
Time, 1949

I'm only scared of three things—lightning, a side-hill putt, and Ben Hogan.

Sam Snead

The answer to Hogan is, I fancy, that if Hogan means to win, you lose.

Henry Longhurst
Round in Sixty-eight, 1953

I've always been friendly with Ben until the past two years or so, I guess, but we haven't had much to do with each other. But, then, Hogan doesn't have much to do with anybody.

Lloyd Mangrum, 1953

Ben wants to know the place so well that he could give a biologist a thorough life history of the four rabbits who hole up off the fourteenth fairway.

Jimmy Demaret
My Partner, Ben Hogan, 1954

"Those steel-gray eyes of his," one friend once remarked with a slight shudder. "He looks at you like a landlord asking for next month's rent."

Will Grimsley
Sport, 1961

All I know is that Nicklaus watches Hogan practice and I never heard of Hogan watching Nicklaus practice.

Tommy Bolt
Golf Digest, 1978

Hale Irwin, American, born 1945

Maybe I'll come out tomorrow on a pogo stick. Maybe they'll notice me then.

Hale Irwin, on his lack of image, 1974

Hale Irwin isn't the sort of golfer who celebrates victories by buying champagne for the house. His idea of a party is drinking a sugar-free cola and contemplating prudent ways of investing his latest paycheck.

Fred Guzman
San Jose Mercury News, 1984

Bobby Jones, American, 1902–1971

They wound up the Mechanical Man of Golf yesterday and sent him clicking round the East Lake course.

Kerr Petrie, on the Southern Open
New York *Herald Tribune*, 1927

One might as well attempt to describe the smoothness of the wind as to paint a clear picture of his complete swing.

Grantland Rice, sportswriter

The steady-going and unimaginative will often beat the more eager champion and they will get very near the top, but there, I think, they will stop. The prose laborer must yield to the poet, and Bobby as a golfer had a strain of poetry in him.

Bernard Darwin, British golf writer

He had supernatural strength of mind.

Ben Hogan

From the time Jones was fourteen to the time he was twenty-eight, no man ever beat him twice in championship match play. . . . To deprecate Jones's record would be a little like saying the Civil War wasn't on the level.

Charles Price
The World of Golf, 1962

Gary Koch, American, born 1952

If that kid ever forgets how to putt, he might as well give up.
> **Peter Cooper, veteran professional on Koch at age sixteen, 1968**

Lawson Little, American, 1910–1968

There were a number of reasons Little's career as a professional was relatively lackluster. . . . After winning a tournament, for one thing, he was often too busy celebrating to win the next one.
> **Charles Price**
> *Golfer-At-Large,* 1982

Gene Littler, American, born 1930

Doesn't take a Rolls Royce long to warm up, does it?
> **Tommy Aaron, watching Littler on the practice tee, 1970**

He gave me a typical Littler conversation. Three yeps, two nopes and two nods.
> **Ted Schroeder, father of pro John Schroeder, 1974**

There's no such guy as Littler. He mails in his scores.
> **Bob Drum, sportswriter, on Littler's image**
> *Golf Digest,* 1975

Bobby Locke, South African, born 1917

He was not like Jack Nicklaus, who careens along the fairways, then takes aeons over the shot. Locke has just two speeds for everything—leisurely and slow.
> **Ken Bowden**
> *Golf Digest,* 1972

That son of a bitch Locke was able to hole a putt over sixty feet of peanut brittle.
> **Lloyd Mangrum**
> *Golf Magazine,* 1982

George Low, American, born 1900?

He is, all at once, America's guest, underground comedian, consultant, inventor of the overlapping grip for a beer can, and, more importantly, a man who has conquered the two hardest things in life—how to putt better than anyone else, and how to live lavishly without an income.
> **Dan Jenkins**
> *The Dogged Victims of Inexorable Fate,* 1970

He was born retired.
> **Jimmy Demaret**

Mark Lye, American, born 1952

Are you guys as surprised as I am?
> **Mark Lye, leading The Masters, to the press, 1984**

Johnny McDermott, American, 1891–1971

For practice McDermott used to hit balls to a newspaper spread out on a field, and the story goes that he sometimes got mad if the ball failed to stop on the right paragraph.
> **Charles Price**
> *The World of Golf,* 1962

Dave Marr, American, born 1933

Some days I felt like Superman and other days I found I was made of Jell-O.
> **Dave Marr**
> *Golf Digest,* 1980

Billy Maxwell, American, born 1929

Billy Maxwell leaps at the ball like a panhandler diving for a
ten-spot.

Tony Lema
Golfer's Gold, 1964

Cary Middlecoff, American, born 1921

Cary, a splendid champion, was forever a slow player. . . .
A joke on the tour used to be that Cary gave up dentistry
because no patient could hold his mouth open that long.

Dan Jenkins
The Dogged Victims of Inexorable Fate, 1970

Middlecoff the dentist, . . . he doesn't hit his irons; he drills
them. . . . Every time he wins another tournament, he raises
his dental rates. We only hope he fills cavities faster than he
plays golf.

Mark Mulvoy and Art Spander
Golf: The Passion and the Challenge, 1977

Johnny Miller, American, born 1947

Schenkel: Johnny Miller has a smooth touch.
Harris: Yeah. As smooth as a man lifting a breast out of an
evening gown.

Chris Schenkel and Phil Harris
"Bing Crosby National Pro-Am," ABC-TV, 1974

Young John is the tour's Mr. Clean. He doesn't smoke, drink,
cuss, or wink at strange girls. He plays pool—but only in
Billy Casper's recreation room.

Dave Hill
Teed Off, 1977

As comfortable in the desert as a cactus.
> **Nick Seitz**
> *Superstars of Golf,* 1978

I had a stretch there for a few years where I played some golf that bordered on the Twilight Zone. . . . I can remember that I was literally getting upset that I had to putt.
> **Johnny Miller, on his play in the mid-1970s**
> *Golf Magazine,* 1982

Orville Moody, American, born 1933

Nor did his cross-handed putting method particularly recommend him, since no man had ever putted cross-handed and won more than a kick in the ass with a cold boot.
> **Dan Jenkins**
> *The Dogged Victims of Inexorable Fate,* 1970

If you had to pick one man you would *not* want putting for your life, he would be it.
> **Bruce Devlin**
> "Seiko-Tucson Match Play Championship,"
> ESPN-TV, 1984

Byron Nelson, American, born 1912

I wouldn't bet *anyone* against Byron Nelson. The only time Nelson left the fairway was to pee in the bushes.
> **Jackie Burke**
> *Golf Magazine,* 1981

Larry Nelson, American, born 1947

Most weeks he couldn't putt the ball into a two-car garage.
> **Dan Lauck**
> *Golf Magazine,* 1984

Jack Nicklaus, American, born 1940

Jack is playing an entirely different game—a game I'm not even familiar with.

Bobby Jones, at The Masters presentation ceremony, 1965

A lot of us [golf fans] never personally liked him. He was the bully on the block who owned the bat and the ball, had the first car, got the first girl; and when he sliced off tackle for twelve yards it always took three of us to drag him down. He was too much.

William Price Fox
Golf Digest, 1973

I said to the writers, "There's Nicklaus, for example, only five strokes back. I wouldn't feel safe from Jack if he was in a wheelchair."

Dan Jenkins
Dead Solid Perfect, 1974

Nicklaus may be the only pro in the world who can frighten other pros with his practice shots.

Dick Schaap
Massacre at Winged Foot, 1974

You worry about Jack when you see him signing up for the tournament.

John Jacobs, at the Bing Crosby National Pro-Am, 1975

I did my best, but chasing Nicklaus is like chasing a walking record book.

Tom Weiskopf, finishing second at The Masters
Golf Digest, 1975

Most of the time he plays with the timidity of a middle-aged spinster walking home through a town full of drunken sailors, always choosing the safe side of the street.
Peter Dobereiner
The Observer (London), 1975

He wouldn't three-putt a supermarket parking lot.
Dave Hill
Teed Off, 1977

When Nicklaus says he has a given number of yards left to the green, . . . believe him. When it comes to shotmaking, he knows everything down to the wind-chill factor.
Mark Mulvoy and Art Spander
Golf: The Passion and the Challenge, 1977

If Nicklaus says an ant can pull a bale of hay, hitch it up. Jack doesn't say anything he doesn't mean and he doesn't know what it is to lie.
Lee Trevino
Golf Digest, 1978

He's a real live wire. His idea of fun is to sit home on a Saturday night with a glass of hot cocoa singing Ohio State fight songs.
Don Rickles, comic

I wouldn't care if I got beat by twenty shots. I'd still like to see how God does it.
Ed Fiori, on being paired with Nicklaus
Golf Digest, 1979

I enjoyed playing in the last group of the day behind Nicklaus. Only trouble was [Tournament Director] Jack Tuthill kept taking the pins off the greens once Nicklaus played through.
Lou Graham
Golf Digest, 1979

Jack Nicklaus has become a legend in his spare time.

Chi Chi Rodriguez
Golf Digest, 1979

To win the things he's won, build golf courses around the world, be a daddy to all those kids, and be a hell of an investor, too, it's phenomenal. Hey, stick a broom in his rear end and he could probably sweep the U.S.A.

Jackie Burke
Golf Magazine, 1981

The difference between Jack and me is that when I got to the top of the mountain in 1974 and 1975, I said, "Hey, it's time to stop and check out the view." Whenever Jack reaches the top of a mountain, he starts looking for another.

Johnny Miller
PGA Tour News, 1983

I never thought his short game was very good. Of course, he hit so many damn greens, it didn't make any difference.

Tom Watson
Golf Digest, 1983

Moe Norman, Canadian, born 1930

The Canadian Moe Norman can not only get the ball up and down from the ball washer, he could, if motivated, play it out of the cup and back *into* the ball washer.

Peter Dobereiner
Golf Digest, 1983

Mac O'Grady, American, born 1951

Anytime you talk to him, you'll hear three words you never heard before.

Mike Nicolette
Sports Illustrated, 1984

Porky Oliver, American, 1916–1961

Porky Oliver, . . . Old Pork Chops—we call him "Corned Beef" now since inflation has changed his eating habits.
Jimmy Demaret
My Partner, Ben Hogan, 1954

Arnold Palmer, American, born 1929

I'll guarantee you he'll get it in the hole if he has to stare it in.
Bob Rosburg, on Palmer's winning putt in The Masters, 1960

Palmer usually walks to the first tee quite unlike any other pro on the circuit. He doesn't walk onto it so much as climb into it, almost as though it were a prize ring; and then he looks around at the gallery as though he is trying to count the house.
Charles Price
The World of Golf, 1962

If Arnold asked all of those people to go jump into the river for him, they would march straight to the river and jump.
Gary Player, on Arnie's Army

Palmer not only makes a golf tournament seem as dangerous as an Indianapolis 500, but he crashes as often as he finishes first.
Mark H. McCormack
Arnie: The Evolution of a Legend, 1967

He first came to golf as a muscular young man who could not keep his shirttail in, who smoked a lot, perspired a lot and who hit the ball with all of the finesse of a dock worker lifting a crate of auto parts.
Dan Jenkins
The Dogged Victims of Inexorable Fate, 1970

He's the reason we're playing for all this money today. Arnie made it all possible. I'll tell you what I think of the man. If he should walk in the door right now and say, "Shine my shoes." I'd take off my shirt, get down on my hands and knees, and shine his shoes.

Ken Still
Golf Magazine, 1970

Golf was a comparatively sexless enterprise before Palmer came a-wooing. His caveman approach took the audience by storm. He was Cagney pushing a grapefruit in Mae Clarke's face, Gable kicking down the door to Scarlett O'Hara's bedroom.

Jim Murray
Los Angeles Times, 1974

Under a new USGA rule, anyone using the word *charisma* in writing about Palmer is henceforth subject to a two-stroke penalty and loss of down.

Herbert Warren Wind
Golf Digest, 1975

It was more fun watching Palmer lose than watching the rest of them win.

Dan Gleason
The Great, The Grand and the Also-Ran, 1976

Like us golfing commoners, he risks looking bad for the sake of some fun.

John Updike
Golf Magazine, 1980

Arnold Palmer had everything except a brake pedal.

Peter Dobereiner
Golf Digest, 1982

He was aggressive. He might be leading by one or two shots but he wouldn't be cautious. He'd go for the flag from the middle of an alligator's back.

Lee Trevino
They Call Me Super Mex, 1982

Jerry Pate, American, born 1953

I'm surprised he didn't drown, because he can't keep his mouth shut.

Jack Nicklaus, after Pate dove into a pond after winning the Memphis Open, 1981

Jerry had everything—from the neck down. With my brains and his swing, we were unbeatable.

Lee Trevino, on his Ryder Cup partner
Golf Digest, 1982

What I can't figure out is, if I'm so dumb, how am I making so much money? Me and Terry Bradshaw, . . . he's so dumb he wins four Super Bowls, and I'm so dumb I'm making a million dollars a year.

Jerry Pate
Inside Sports, 1982

Billy Joe Patton, American, born 1922

He was always "up." If he wasn't talking, you knew he was ill.

Jack Nicklaus
The Greatest Game of All, 1969

Bareheaded, bespectacled, grinning, with a faster swing than a kitchen blender.

Dan Jenkins
The Dogged Victims of Inexorable Fate, 1970

Corey Pavin, American, born 1959

Corey is a little on the slight side. When he goes through a turnstile, nothing happens.

Jim Moriarty
Golf Digest, 1984

Calvin Peete, American, born 1943

He has a crooked left arm—until he reaches out for the paycheck.

Lee Trevino, on Peete's elbow injury
San Francisco Examiner, 1983

Gary Player, South African, born 1935

He was very mystical, a health fanatic who was big on the power of positive thinking. . . . Were he to land in hell, his critics said, he would probably immediately start talking about what a wonderful place it is.

Dan Gleason
The Great, The Grand and the Also-Ran, 1976

He runs and lifts weights and eats health foods. That's all well and good, but I get tired of hearing him brag about it. So what if he has the most perfect bowel movements on the tour?

Dave Hill
Teed Off, 1977

Gary Player is all right if you like to see a grown man dressed up like Black Bart all the time.

Don Rickles, comic

Playing against him, you begin hoping he'll be on grass rather than in sand. From grass you expect him to pitch the ball close. From a bunker you're afraid he'll hole it out!

Jack Nicklaus
Golf Magazine, 1982

Phil Rodgers, American, born 1938

In my next life, I'd like to be an otter. They only do two things—eat abalone and play.

Phil Rodgers
Golf Digest, 1983

Chi Chi Rodriguez, Puerto Rican, born 1935

You should have seen how little I was as a kid. I was so small that I got my start in golf as a ball marker.

Chi Chi Rodriguez, 1971

I'm going for the flag today. I'm gonna be a firecracker out there. I'm gonna be so hot they're gonna be playing on brown fairways tomorrow.

Chi Chi Rodriguez, at the U.S. Open, 1974

He hits the ball so straight. It's from hitting it in those Puerto Rican alleys.

Dave Stockton, at the Everett Open, 1984

Paul Runyan, American, born 1908

Watch Paul's unhurried swing. It's as lazy as a Spanish siesta, as delicately fashioned as a flower petal.

Horton Smith

Doug Sanders, American, born 1933

Doug Sanders braces himself with a wide stance that looks like a sailor leaning into a northeast gale.

Tony Lema
Golfer's Gold, 1964

Doug Sanders has said he likes to have sex and a hot tub bath every morning and he's loose and ready to go. Of course, if Sanders had scored half as often with women as he claims he has, he'd be dead.

Dave Hill
Teed Off, 1977

Emmett Kelly picks out his clothes. Smart outfits. Doug looks like he took a bad trip through a paint factory.

Don Rickles, comedian

He had the flashiest clothes and the flashiest women. . . . I spent a night in his place in Dallas once. All he had in it was booze and about a hundred and fifty pairs of golf shoes.

Lee Trevino
They Call Me Super Mex, 1982

Because of his world-famous color-coordinated outfits, . . . Doug has been described as looking like the aftermath of a direct hit on a pizza factory.

Dave Marr
Golf Digest, 1983

He is a dashing Southerner with a fetching smile and a ready eye for the ladies. Put him on the North Pole and he'll have every Eskimo around at a party within twenty-four hours.

Dan Hruby
San Jose Mercury News, 1984

Gene Sarazen, American, born 1902

Heck, if it wasn't for golf, Sarazen would be back on a banana boat between Naples and Sicily.

Jimmy Demaret

John Schroeder, American, born 1945

Hey, Schroeder, you're gonna be the first guy ever penalized for slow play in a driving contest.

A pro, quoted in
Golf Digest, 1974

Charlie Sifford, American, born 1923

His swing is nothing to go home and press in the leaves of the family Bible. There are days when he could putt better with a rake.

Jim Murray
The Sporting World of Jim Murray, 1968

The first time I played here, back in 1959, I'll never forget it. People looked at me as if I had a tail.

Charlie Sifford, on being an early black golfer at the U.S. Open at Winged Foot, 1974

Sifford was a very talented player whose trademark cigar seemed to be eternally short, perhaps because he got so many doors slammed in his face.

Dan Gleason
The Great, The Grand and the Also-Ran, 1976

Dan Sikes, American, born 1930

Before entering professional golf, Dan was a lawyer, which may possibly explain why he doesn't feel right unless he's complaining about something.

Jack Nicklaus
The Greatest Game of All, 1969

Macdonald Smith, American, 1890–1949

He has the cleanest twenty-one-jewel stroke in golf. He treats the grass of a golf course as though it were an altar cloth.

Tommy Armour
The American Golfer, 1935

J.C. Snead, American, born 1941

When J.C. was a kid, he was so ugly, they had to tie a pork chop around his neck to get the dog to play with him.

Lee Trevino
Golf Digest, 1978

Sam Snead, American, born 1912

At the start, Sam Snead was a simple lad who couldn't tell the time in a clock factory.

Herb Graffis, golf writer and editor

The only difference in Snead is that he's gettin' humpbacked from pickin' balls out of the can.

Jimmy Demaret, on Snead's comeback, 1949

Where I lived, near Bald Knob, the roads got littler and littler until they just ran up a tree. Big cities were something I'd just heard rumors about.

Sam Snead
The Education of a Golfer, 1962

It's called color. Some people have it and some don't. As for Slammin' Sam Snead, he has enough color to outfit a couple of rainbow factories.

Rex Lardner
The Great Golfers, 1970

Sam Snead's got more money buried underground than I ever made on top. . . . He's got gophers in his backyard that subscribe to *Fortune* magazine. He's packed more coffee cans than Brazil.

> **Arnold Palmer**
> "Chrysler Presents a Bob Hope Special," NBC-TV, 1963

Any guy who would pass up a chance to see Sam Snead play golf would pull the shades driving past the Taj Mahal.

> **Jim Murray**
> *The Sporting World of Jim Murray*, 1968

While he has yet to read *War and Peace*, Snead wasn't any more a hillbilly than Shirley Temple was a midget.

> **Charles Price**
> *Golf Digest*, 1983

Craig Stadler, American, born 1953

How can I not like Craig? He's the best thing that ever happened to me. He makes me look good.

> **Tom Weiskopf, on Stadler's temper**
> *Sports Illustrated*, 1982

Some guys hope to shoot their age. Craig Stadler hopes to shoot his waist.

> **Jim Murray**
> *Los Angeles Times*, 1980

Hal Sutton, American, born 1958

If God were a teenager and descended to give us the Word, He'd probably look like Hal Sutton.

> **Nathaniel Crosby**
> *Golf Magazine*, 1983

Jerry Travers, American, 1887–1951

Travers was the greatest competitor I have ever known. I could always tell just from looking at a golfer whether he was winning or losing, but I *never* knew how Travers stood.

Alex Smith, Scottish professional

Walter J. Travis, Australian, 1862–1927

Travis holed out from such immeasurable distances that his opponents claimed he could putt the eyes out of a chipmunk. . . . Travis could go weeks without missing a fairway and play through a hurricane wearing a ten-gallon hat.

Charles Price
Golfer-At-Large, 1982

Lee Trevino, American, born 1939

If he didn't have an Adam's apple he'd have no shape at all.

Gary Player
Sports Illustrated, 1972

He's the only man I've ever known to talk on his backswing.

Charley McClendon, LSU football coach
Sports Illustrated, 1972

He knows how to live. The breweries will have to go on overtime while he is in the money, and everybody had better lock up their daughters.

Peter Dobereiner
Golf World, 1973

I can't keep my mouth shut for four hours around a golf course. If I did, I'd get bad breath.

Lee Trevino
Golf Digest, 1974

Lee's got more lines than the Illinois Railroad.
                                    Fuzzy Zoeller
                                    San Francisco Chronicle, 1979

I'm very lucky. If it wasn't for golf I don't know what I'd be doing. If my IQ had been two points lower, I'd have been a plant somewhere.
                                    Lee Trevino
                                    They Call Me Super Mex, 1982

Harry Vardon, British, 1870–1937

At that time, Vardon was the most atrocious putter I have ever seen. He didn't three putt, he *four*-putted.
                    Gene Sarazen, on Vardon in the early 1920s

The groove in his swing was so obvious you could almost see it. I was so impressed that during the last round, when my swing started to leave me, I started imitating his. And it worked, too. Fact is, I almost caught him with his own swing.
                              Walter Hagen, on the 1913 U.S. Open

A grand player up to the green, and a very bad player when he got there. But then, Vardon gave himself less putting to do than any other man.
                              Bernard Darwin, British golf writer

He would not play any course twice in the same day, you know. Why not? Because he was so accurate, that in his second round his shots finished in the divot holes he had made in the morning, and that took the fun out of the game for him.
                                    Henry Cotton
                                    Country Life, 1948

He held on to the club as though it were a garden rake, addressed it as though he were about to pick up a piano, and swung at it as though he were trying to get out of the way of something.

Charles Price
Golfer-At-Large, 1982

Lanny Wadkins, American, born 1949

He's the most tenacious player I've ever seen. You put a pin in the middle of a lake and Lanny will attack it.

John Mahaffey
Golf Digest, 1983

Lanny is a self-confessed optimist, the kind who, if he falls in a sewer, checks his pockets for fish.

Mickey Herskowitz
Golf Digest, 1983

Lanny is back home in Maine painting his house. As fast as he does everything, what's he going to do on the second day?
Dan Jenkins
"PGA Highlights," ESPN-TV, 1985

Tom Watson, American, born 1949

Watson walks about his golf-course business like a young trial lawyer going from one courtroom to the next.
Al Barkow
Golf's Golden Grind, 1974

Watson scares me. If he's lying six in the middle of the fairway, there's some kind of way he might make a five.
Lee Trevino
San Francisco Chronicle, 1979

Tom Watson is a hell of a golfer, but he sure could use a choreographer. Watching him shoot sixty-six is like watching the President sign a bill.

Jay Cronley
Playboy, 1981

Watson's close friends enjoy describing him as "the worst walker and worst dresser in golf."

Herbert Warren Wind
The New Yorker, 1981

Any self-respecting tournament wants to be won by Tom Watson.

Jim Murray
Golf Magazine, 1983

When you drive into the left rough, hack your second out into a greenside bunker, come out within six feet of the hole and sink the slippery putt—when you do that, you've made a Watson par.

Andy Bean
Golf Digest, 1984

Tom Weiskopf, American, born 1942

Tom Weiskopf is getting ready to issue his first quote of the year, and I don't want to miss it.

Dan Jenkins
Sports Illustrated, 1971

His swing was made in heaven, part velvet, part silk, like a royal robe, so sweet you could pour it over ice cream.

Jim Murray
Los Angeles Times

He knows more ways of choking than Dracula.

Colman McCarthy
The Pleasures of the Game, 1977

I'm not an intellectual person. I don't get headaches from concentration. I get them from double bogeys.

Tom Weiskopf
Golf Digest, 1978

Willie Wood, American, born 1960

In the tour media guide, Wood's height is given at five feet seven inches, presumably on an elevated tee. His weight should be listed as 135/11/25—which is 135 pounds the day after Thanksgiving.

Jim Moriarty
Golf Digest, 1984

Kermit Zarley, American, born 1941

The pro from the moon.

Bob Hope

Fuzzy Zoeller, American, born 1951

Zoeller turned pro in 1975 and, for a while, did his very best to drink all the tour stops dry and accommodate as many beautiful galleryites as humanly possible.

Maury White
Des Moines Register, 1979

When I catch my driver and Fuzzy catches his one-iron, I can get within thirty yards of him.

Hale Irwin
Sports Illustrated, 1981

When your name is Zoeller, and so many things are done in alphabetical order, you expect to be last.

Fuzzy Zoeller

Maybe Fuzzy Zoeller plays golf the way everybody should. Hit it, go find it, hit it again. Grin, have a smoke, take a sip, make a joke and every so often win a major championship.

Dan Jenkins
Sports Illustrated, 1984

36. Tour Players: Women

Amy Alcott, American, born 1956

It's easy to be liked if you're 100th on the money list. You may have to worry about making ends meet but everyone will love you.

Amy Alcott, on her image among fellow players
Golf Digest, 1984

Pat Bradley, American, born 1951

I swear, I'm the queen of the lip-out and the rim-out. The ball comes out, and looks at me and grins as if to say, "Too bad. You missed again."

Pat Bradley
Golf Digest, 1979

JoAnne Carner, American, born 1939

The ground shakes when she hits it.

Sandra Palmer, who nicknamed Carner "Big Mama"
Sports Illustrated, 1982

Her weight is a state secret.

John P. May
Golf Digest, 1982

We have so many small players out here on tour, that's why I look like Big Mama.

JoAnne Carner
"LPGA Kemper Open," NBC-TV, 1983

The only thing I never learned from Billy Martin was how to knock a guy out in a bar.

JoAnne Carner, who says the Yankees manager taught her how to win

Beth Daniel, American, born 1956

Chasing Beth is like swimming upstream against the current.

Bonnie Lauer, at the Birmingham Classic, 1982

Sally Little, American, born 1951

I kept seeing her ass all day, bending over to pick her ball out of the hole.

Hollis Stacy, on Little's closing sixty-four in the Nabisco Dinah Shore Invitational
Sports Illustrated, 1982

Nancy Lopez, American, born 1957

They've got the wrong person playing Wonder Woman on television.

Judy Rankin
Golf Digest, 1978

We're all trying to steal Nancy's birth-control pills, but so far we've been unsuccessful.

> **JoAnne Carner**
> *Golf Digest,* 1980

She just goes to prove that golf is not a hard game to learn. Her old man could fix a fender in the morning and teach her how to play golf in the afternoon.

> **Herb Graffis**
> *Golf Digest,* 1981

My swing is no uglier than Arnold Palmer's, and it's the same ugly swing every time.

> **Nancy Lopez**
> *Golf Digest,* 1984

Patty Sheehan, American, born 1956

I need five weeks off. Everybody keeps telling me how great I am. I can't be a jerk even if I want to, and it's driving me nuts.

> **Patty Sheehan**
> *Sports Illustrated,* 1984

It's nice to have the opportunity to play for so much money, but it's nicer to win it.

> **Patty Sheehan**
> *Golf Magazine,* 1985

Muffin Spencer-Devlin, American, born 1953

Oh, no. I've been at it much too long and have too much experience. I'd say I'm a Space Captain.

> **Muffin Spencer-Devlin, asked if she was a Space Cadet**
> *San Francisco Examiner,* 1982

When I was born, they had to use forceps and there were indentations in my forehead. My grandmother said, "Why, she looks just like a little muffin!"

Muffin Spencer-Devlin, on how she got the name Muffin, Safeco Classic, 1984

Now I've got to call my editor and ask for more space. . . . Where would we have been for three days without her?

Lynn Mucken, *Seattle Times* golf writer, after listening to Spencer-Devlin's tales at the Safeco Classic, 1984

Sandra Spuzich, American, born 1937

Maybe she's starting a new trend in golf—no practice. The only exercise Spooz gets before a round is swinging that weighted donut on her driver.

JoAnne Carner
Golf Digest, 1983

Hollis Stacy, American, born 1954

Shirttail hanging out, hair blowing in the wind, dragging on a cigarette. That's sex appeal.

Arnold Palmer, 1981

Jan Stephenson, Australian, born 1951

I may not be the prettiest girl in the world, but I'd like to see Bo Derek rate a "10" after playing 18 holes in 100-degree heat.

Jan Stephenson, on hearing a writer rated her a "6"
San Jose Mercury News, 1981

Hell, if I were built like Jan I'd show it off, too.

JoAnne Carner
Golf Digest, 1982

Glenna Collett Vare, American, born 1903

No one else quite so adequately expressed how far women's golf had come since those far-off days when women swung at the ball as though they were beating off purse-snatchers with an umbrella.

Charles Price
The World of Golf, 1962

Joyce Wethered, British, born 1901

Good *swing*? My god, mon! She could hit a ball 240 yards on the fly while standing barefoot on a cake of ice.

Willie Wilson, Scottish professional

Mickey Wright, American, born 1935

We had some great head-to-head matches. Nine times out of ten, she won.

Kathy Whitworth
Golf Magazine, 1983

Babe Didrikson Zaharias, American, 1914–1956

If ah didn't have these ah'd hit it twenty yards farther.

Babe Didrikson Zaharias, on her breasts

There's only one thing wrong about Babe and me. I hit the ball like a girl and she hits like a man.

Bob Hope, c. 1940s

37. Winning and Losing

If you hear a man complaining of having "lost all interest" in a match which he has lately played, you will be pretty safe in inferring that he lost it. The winner very seldom experiences this feeling.

Horace G. Hutchinson
Hints on the Game of Golf, 1886

Given an equality of strength and skill, the victory in golf will be to him who is captain of his soul. Give me a clear eye, a healthy liver, a strong will, a collected mind, and a conscience void of offense both toward God and toward man, and I will back the pigmy against the giant.

Arnold Haultain
Atlantic Monthly, 1908

The one stroke marks the difference between fame and oblivion.

Samuel L. Parrish, USGA treasurer
The American Golfer, 1929

The life of a professional athlete is precarious at best. Win and they carry you to the clubhouse on their shoulders; lose and you pay the caddies in the dark.

Gene Sarazen
Thirty Years of Championship Golf, 1950

In order to win you must play your best golf when you need it most, and play your sloppy stuff when you can afford it. I shall not attempt to explain how you achieve this happy timing.

Bobby Jones
Golf Is My Game, 1960

It seems paradoxical, but it is probably true that the way to obtain a great reputation as a fighter is to forget that you have an enemy—or at any rate an earthly one.

Bernard Darwin, writing about Bobby Jones

I wouldn't hurt a chicken crossing the road, but if I got a man in trouble on the golf course I'd kick the hell out of him. I don't care if he's my best friend.

Sam Snead
Golf Digest, 1972

Before the last round I called my wife and told her I had a seventeen-stroke lead over last place.

Rod Funseth, leading the Glen Campbell–Los Angeles Open, 1973

I really don't like playoffs. I feel sorry for the other guy if I win and I feel worse if I lose.

Chi Chi Rodriguez
Golf Digest, 1974

Youngster: Well, if you don't win, how come you're a pro?
Shaw: You've got a good point.

Tom Shaw, at the U.S. Open, 1974

I prefer to think of it as fourth.

Hale Irwin, finishing last in the World Series of Golf
Golf Digest, 1974

People don't seem to realize how often you have to come in second in order to finish first. . . . I've never met a winner who hadn't learned how to be a loser.

Jack Nicklaus, who has finished second over fifty-five times
Golf Magazine, 1976

Nicklaus exudes the killer instinct peculiar to sports immortals. The breakfast of champions is not cereal, it's your opposition.

Nick Seitz
PGA Tour Annual, 1977

I can't describe how I feel. It's the greatest thing in the world to win a professional golf tournament—especially if you're a professional golfer.

Dave Eichelberger, upon winning the Milwaukee Open
Golf Digest, 1977

The difference between shooting a sixty-three and a seventy-three might even be just between your ears. It's such a fine line that it's almost scary.

Johnny Miller
San Francisco Chronicle, 1979

Most golfers prepare for disaster. A good golfer prepares for success.

Bob Toski
Golf Digest, 1981

The arc of your swing doesn't have a thing to do with the size of your heart.

Carol Mann
Newsweek, 1981

If you aspire to be a champion, it's up to you to find a way to get the ball in the cup on the crucial holes on the last day.

Tom Watson
The New Yorker, 1981

Ah, well. If we hit it perfect every day, everybody else would quit.

> **Lee Trevino, to Tom Watson**
> *Esquire,* 1982

Show me someone who gets angry once in a while, and I'll show you a guy with a killer instinct. Show me a guy walking down the fairway smiling and I'll show you a loser.

> **Lee Trevino**
> "Bob Hope Classic," NBC-TV, 1983

Winning is the greatest feeling. It's like walking barefoot in the mud.

> **Lynn Adams, upon winning the Orlando Classic**
> *Golf Digest,* 1983

Victory is everything. You can spend the money, but you can never spend the memories.

> **Ken Venturi**
> "Colonial National Invitation," CBS-TV, 1983

If you want to whip somebody on the golf course, just get him mad.

> **Dave Williams, University of Houston golf coach**
> *Golf Magazine,* 1984

If you ever feel sorry for somebody on a golf course, you better go home. If you don't kill them, they'll kill you.

> **Seve Ballesteros**
> *Seve: The Young Champion,* 1984

38. Women

Three things are as unfathomable as they are fascinating to the masculine mind: metaphysics, golf, and the feminine heart.

Arnold Haultain
The Mystery of Golf, 1908

Call every woman "Sugar" and you can't go wrong.

Walter Hagen

During the last three holes of the 1919 U.S. Open, which The Haig won for the second time, he smiled at a pretty girl on the sixteenth tee, struck up a conversation with her on the seventeenth fairway, and made a date with her as he walked off the eighteenth green. After The Haig, nobody would take golf *too* seriously.

Charles Price

Love has had a lot of press-agenting from the oldest times; but there are higher, nobler things than love. A woman is only a woman, but a hefty drive is a slosh.

P. G. Wodehouse
"A Woman Is Only a Woman," 1919

His handicap was down to twelve. But these things are not all. A golfer needs a loving wife, to whom he can describe the day's play through the long evenings.

P. G. Wodehouse

Joe Bean says one thing about caddying for these dames, it keeps you out of the hot sun. . . . And another time he said that it was not fair to charge these dames regular ladies' dues in the club as they hardly ever used the course.

Ring Lardner
"A Caddy's Diary," 1922

If your wife interferes with your golf, get a new wife. If your business interferes with your golf, get a new business.

Don Herold
Love That Golf, 1952

He married the first girl who would shag balls for him.

George Low, on Arnold Palmer, 1955

Golf and sex are about the only things you can enjoy without being good at it.

Jimmy Demaret

Golf is a diabolical contrivance, but it is not so devilish as the woman scorned for a driving range.

Milton Gross
Eighteen Holes in My Head, 1959

Aware of their long life expectancy, they play slowly, hunt for a ball for twenty minutes and permutate their scores the way they figure out who has to pay for what after lunch at Schrafft's.

Rex Lardner, on women golfers
Out of the Bunker and Into the Trees, 1960

I've always had a wife—golf. No man should have more than one.

Freddie McLeod, American pro, on why he never married

I'll buy me another wife.

> **Peter Thomson, Australian pro, asked what he'd do with his money**

Oh, man, Mary Rose worked me so hard at home that I had to come back out on the tour to get my health back.

> **Johnny Pott, on his wife**

Jack, you spent more time in the recovery room than your wife did.

> **Dr. William Copeland, to Jack Nicklaus on the birth of his first child, 1963**

When I come back in the next life, I want to come back as a golf pro's wife. She wakes up every morning at the crack of ten, and is faced by her first major decision of the day: whether to have breakfast in bed or in the hotel coffee shop.

> **Dan Sikes, American touring professional**

When we were really kids out there, it was great. But the longer you stay out, the more ding-a-lings you find. Really. There are just too many places, like Palm Springs, that are dingy. They bell me out.

> **Susan Marr, wife of touring pro Dave Marr, 1968**

I wasn't taking much of a risk—I knew she was a beauty queen.

> **Dave Stockton, on the blind date with his future wife**
> *Golf Digest,* 1970

This guy has fifteen kids. *Bleeped* himself right out of a seat in the car.

> **Ben Hogan, on a restaurant manager**
> *Golf Digest,* 1970

I have to win this tournament. My wife bought $50,000 worth of furniture last week. And you should see the house she built around it.

Lee Trevino, at the U.S. Open, 1974

"A bad wife'll strap a terminal hook on you," Donny said once. "You can just start walking left every time you swing the club."

Dan Jenkins
Dead Solid Perfect, 1974

Golf may have driven more people crazy than women.

Dan Jenkins
Dead Solid Perfect, 1974

Hawaii has so many girls on the island. You've got to weigh that. And let's not sell Jacksonville short. Jacksonville, as a matter of fact, is the only place where the girls find out where you're staying and call *you*.

John Jacobs, on the best tour stops, 1975

He looks for 'em in the gallery, and man, he spots one, we gotta lose three strokes.

Doug Sanders' caddie, on women at tournaments

Shorts and a tight sweater have caused more guys to bogey a hole than a bad slice.

Jim Murray
The Sporting World of Jim Murray, 1968

Question: Is golf better than booze and broads?
Demaret: I don't know about you, young fellow, but I've been playing golf man and boy for thirty-four years—to get money for booze and broads.

Jimmy Demaret

She said, "Oh, I'm so excited! I've never been on a par five in two before. If I sink this putt, it'll be my first eagle! I'll kill myself!" Her husband said, "It's a gimmie."

Buddy Hackett
The Truth About Golf and Other Lies, 1968

He overheard one guy say: "I just got a new set of clubs for my wife." And the other replied: "Now that's what I call a real good trade."

Joe Chase, Plantation Golf Club professional
Golf Magazine, 1970

If he had a job as an accountant, I wouldn't go down to watch him work.

Leslie Thompson, on why she doesn't follow her husband Leonard on tour, 1975

If he [the golf pro] could qualify for the Colonial Open in Fort Worth, Texas, a hunch-backed cyclops could leave the grounds with a pretty girl.

Dan Gleason
The Great, The Grand and the Also-Ran, 1976

To me getting laid is no major accomplishment. While I am getting laid, probably four hundred million other people around the world are getting laid, too. Big deal. I've never found sex that exciting, not nearly as exciting as golf.

Dave Hill
Teed Off, 1977

On Mother's Day, she ain't my mother, so I ain't going to get her nothing.

Lee Trevino, on gifts for his wife
Golf Magazine, 1977

I was playing once with the King of Samoa. I asked him what his handicap was. "Six wives," he said.

Jack Redmond, American trick-shot artist
Golf Digest, 1977

I've always had three rules for playing well on the tour: no push-ups, no swimming and no sex after Wednesday.

Sam Snead
Golf Digest, 1977

Nuthin' on the planet smart as a woman. . . . There's no foolin' round they don't know about! Let me tell ya, baby! No corporation, no government, no anything can check and collect like they can! No way!

Lee Trevino
Golf Digest, 1978

My wife doesn't care what I do when I'm away, as long as I don't have a good time.

Lee Trevino

He's a newlywed, and he might be thinking, "Honey, I just hit our new freezer into the lake at twelve."

Dave Marr, commentator
ABC-TV, 1978

You women want equality, but you'll never get it because women are inferior to men in all sorts of ways—physically, intellectually, and morally. There are exceptions, but on the whole women are inferior to men.

Seve Ballesteros
El Pais (Madrid), 1980

We took a mulligan.

Cheryl Kratzert, wife of Bill, on their divorce and remarriage
Sports Illustrated, 1981

Son, the only way to forget a woman is with another one.

Lee Trevino, quoting his grandfather
They Call Me Super Mex, 1982

At a press conference someone asked me if I brought my wife. "Naw," I said. "You don't bring a ham sandwich to a banquet!"

Lee Trevino, at a party-filled San Antonio tournament
They Call Me Super Mex, 1982

I'm asked all the time what my secret is. "The only secrets I have," I say, "are the ones I keep from my wife."

Bob Toski, teaching professional
Golf Digest, 1982

My enthusiasm for the game has dwindled in that I've found something more interesting than golf—a wife.

Bruce Lietzke, 1982

You take twenty senior events and fifteen regular tour events and what you've got is a divorce.

Miller Barber
Sports Illustrated, 1982

I'm not winning, but I think my ex-wife is the twelfth leading money winner on tour.

Rex Caldwell
Golf Digest, 1983

My wife's idea of camping out is staying at the Marriott or Howard Johnson's.

Johnny Miller
Golf Digest, 1983

I've been cooking his eggs for thirty years, and he still thinks he has to be in the kitchen telling me how to do it.

Winnie Palmer, on husband Arnold
Golf Magazine, 1983

It's the first job he's had since I married him.

Jeanne Weiskopf, on husband Tom's job as a course designer
Golf Digest, 1983

It was a complete surprise to me, but, on the other hand, it didn't surprise me at all. That'll happen when you haven't been home in eighteen years.

Lee Trevino, on his divorce
Washington Post, 1983

Same name, that way I won't forget it. And I don't have to change the towels. I got a $1.4 million home with my initials all over it, so I might as well live with someone whose name begins with a C.

Lee Trevino, on his second wife, also named Claudia
San Jose Mercury News, 1983

39. Women's Tour

You trying to ask me do I wear girdles and bras and the rest of that junk? What do you think I am? A sissy?

Babe Didrikson Zaharias, c. 1940s

Look at him! When I married him, he was a Greek God. Now he's a big fat Greek.

Babe Didrikson Zaharias, on her husband George

Just ask yourself how good Nicklaus would be if he had to do his nails and put up his hair every night before a tournament? Could he shoot sixty-eight if he was trying to make up his mind which dress to wear to the party that night?

Jim Murray
The Sporting World of Jim Murray, 1968

Nope. I got my period.

Donna Caponi, asked if she choked, 1969

Before that tournament started I wrote six things in lipstick on the mirror. . . . They were six things I wanted to do with my game. By the time the week was over I hadn't done any of them—and I'd added three more!

JoAnne Carner, at the U.S. Women's Open
Golf Digest, 1971

Where I came from, a so-called lady golfer was always something to be hollered at, like an overheating '53 Buick blocking traffic, or a sullen waitress who couldn't remember to put cheese on the 'burger and leave off the onions. . . . That's how it was growing up back in Texas.

Dan Jenkins
Sports Illustrated, 1971

Janie did nothing irregular that I know of. If I had thought she did, I would have grabbed her by the pigtails and slapped her ass.

Lenny Wirtz, former LPGA executive director, on the Blalock cheating incident, 1972

The Ladies Professional Golfers Association did build a fairly busy tournament circuit, and has in recent years grown to where the women play for over a million dollars in . . . can we call it purse money?

Al Barkow
Golf's Golden Grind, 1974

When you first start on the tour, you do a lot of sightseeing. But after you've seen the Alamo five times, what do you do?

Jan Ferraris
Wall Street Journal, 1975

It's still a financial struggle. The sixtieth woman player in 1974 made exactly $5,071.25, and probably used the twenty-five cents to do her own laundry.

Dan Gleason
The Great, The Grand and the Also-Ran, 1976

If it weren't for golf, I'd be waiting on this table instead of sitting at it.

Judy Rankin
Golf Digest, 1977

After a tournament, I'll usually pile into a car with a bunch of girls, and we'll go out and drink beer at some sleazy bar. You know, once in a while I'll get lucky.

McLean Stevenson, on his backing of the LPGA
Golf Magazine, 1977

What we need is less leg and more length. . . . We have too many players thinking about diets and getting their hair curled.

Debbie Massey
Golf Digest, 1979

After seeing Amy Alcott in the Women's U.S. Open on TV, I was impressed with how she kissed her caddie when she won. My next move is to fire my caddie and find me one I can kiss.

Lou Graham
San Jose Mercury News, 1980

Look like a woman, but play like a man.

Jan Stephenson
Golf Magazine, 1981

I have a pilot's license myself, and I don't fly into those big airports. I fly into those little ones, where I can just get on the radio and say, "Here I come so get out of the way."

Jerilyn Britz
Golf Digest, 1981

Now I don't dare throw a club.

JoAnne Carner, on winning the Bob Jones Award for sportsmanship, 1981

The pleasure derived from hitting the ball dead center on the club is comparable only to one or two other pleasures that come to mind at the moment.

Dinah Shore
Golf Magazine, 1981

Dinah's a great gal. . . . One year she let me play in the tournament on Thursday and I was leading after five holes. Then my wig fell off and they discovered I wasn't Sandra Palmer.

Bob Hope
Golf Digest, 1981

The LPGA needs a player that looks like Farrah Fawcett and plays like Jack Nicklaus. Instead, they've got players who look like Jack Nicklaus and play like Farrah Fawcett.

Anon, quoted in
Golf Digest, 1981

Is our organization so unaware of the real glamour and attraction staring it in the face that it must resort to such trash.

Jane Blalock, on the pin-up feature in the LPGA's *Fairway* magazine, 1981

I didn't join the Tour to be in a chorus line.
> **Kathy Whitworth, on the *Fairway* flap**
> *Golf Magazine*, 1981

When my mother saw the slides, she asked, "How did they get your face on Betty Grable's body?"
> **Muffin Spencer-Devlin, on her pinup picture in the LPGA magazine**
> *The Sporting News*, 1982

I keep telling them that they need a little cellulite—a Miss Piggy of the LPGA.
> **JoAnne Carner, on posing for the pinup section of the LPGA's *Fairway* magazine**
> *Orlando Sentinel*, 1982

He quit playing when I started outdriving him.
> **JoAnne Carner, on her husband Don**
> *Sports Illustrated*, 1982

I visualize hitting the ball as far as JoAnne Carner, putting like Amy Alcott, looking like Jan Stephenson and having Carol Mann's husband.
> **Dinah Shore**
> *Des Moines Register*, 1982

Larry doesn't do the logical thing. He doesn't do things like a man. He fights like a woman. He won't fight fair.
> **Jan Stephenson, on her estranged husband Larry Kolb**
> *Golf Digest*, 1982

He's worse than John Hinckley. He thinks I'm his Jodie Foster.
> **Jan Stephenson, on Kolb**
> *Sports Illustrated*, 1982

Jan is no more responsible for her actions than Patty Hearst was when she was calling her parents "Pigs" and shooting up banks with machine guns.

Larry Kolb, on Stephenson
Sports Illustrated, 1982

The real story is that he's an idiot and I dumped him.

Jan Stephenson, on Kolb
Dallas Morning News, 1982

The subjects guaranteed to get the most ink in women's golf are pornography, marriage and divorce, and homosexuality.

Ray Volpe, LPGA Commissioner
Oui, 1982

When they were awarding a car for a hole-in-one on a certain hole, I hit a four-wood . . . and my ball bounced onto the hood of the car. Someone told me, "I don't think you understand. You have to hit the hole, not the car."

Mary Dwyer
Golf Digest, 1982

I've quit worrying about poor shots. I just tell myself, "Relax, Bozo. If you can't have fun, you shouldn't be out here."

Patty Sheehan, 1982

Women Who Seek Equality With Men Lack Ambition.

Patty Sheehan, bumper sticker on her car
The Sporting News, 1983

Instead of my yardage book, I was reaching for my flight guide.

JoAnne Carner, upon shooting an eighty-one
Sports Illustrated, 1983

I went into a dry cleaning store and the guy asked me what I did for a living. I told him I was a professional golfer and he said, "Oh, only Nancy Lopez makes any money."

Hollis Stacy
San Francisco Chronicle, 1983

I've had sex in a lot of places. I wouldn't want to have it in the bunker, because of the sand. I'd kind of like to have it on the green; it would be nice and soft.

Jan Stephenson
Playboy, 1983

I'll take the two-stroke penalty, but I'll be damned if I'll play it where it lays.

Elaine Johnson, Canadian amateur golfer, as her ball landed in her bra
Sports Illustrated, 1983

It's a hard way to make an easy living.

Joyce Kazmierski, winless on the LPGA tour for fourteen years
Golf Digest, 1983

I was concentrating so hard on that putt I forgot what was going on.

Cathy Mant, missing a birdie putt, 1984

What club? A putter.

Ayako Okamoto, when asked what club she used to birdie a hole, 1984

I was a cheerleader in seventh grade and hated it. . . . I wanted to be out there on the field playing and competing, not on the sidelines bouncing around.

Juli Inkster
Seattle Post-Intelligencer, 1984

I'm getting serious about my career because I'm going to be a mother. My dog is pregnant.

Muffin Spencer-Devlin, at the Safeco Classic, 1984

I don't remember too much about it. One hour after I finished, I was drunk.

Penny Pulz, on winning the 1979 Corning Classic
Golf World, 1984

I do all the endorsements because I'm the one they want. Pat Bradley is a great player, but what can you say about Pat Bradley but what she shot? All she does is practice and play.

Jan Stephenson, at the Virginia Bank Classic, 1984

Them two [Pat Bradley and Jan Stephenson] don't get along. It's like the Celtics playing the Lakers. Whenever they're matched, they both shoot well because they hate each other.

Jerry Woodard, Bradley's caddie
Sports Illustrated, 1985

40. Woods and Irons

All those who drive thirty yards suppose themselves to be great *putters*.

Sir Walter Simpson
The Art of Golf, 1887

There's ninety ways to get out of the rough after a long drive, but no way at all to pick up those yards you've lost by hitting them soft.

Sam Snead, advice to Johnny Weismuller, 1947

I hit a hook that went so far out of bounds I almost killed a horse in some stables a cab ride from the first fairway. I was so nervous I didn't have the strength to push the tee in the ground.

Mike Souchak, on beginning his career at the Los Angeles Open

The only fun in the game is watching the ball fly through the air.

Jackie Burke

What other people may find in poetry or art museums, I find in the flight of a good drive.

Arnold Palmer
My Game and Yours, 1965

Anytime a golfer hits a ball perfectly straight with a big club it is, in my view, a fluke.

Jack Nicklaus

I'll take anything in the air that doesn't sting.

Dave Marr, 1968

If your caddie coaches you on the tee, "Hit it down the left side with a little draw," ignore him. All you do on the tee is try not to hit the caddie.

Jim Murray
The Sporting World of Jim Murray, 1968

It may have been the greatest four-wood anyone ever hit. It was so much on the flag that I had to lean sideways to follow the flight of the ball.

Gary Player, to the press

I once hit a drive five hundred yards—on a par-three hole. I had a three-wood coming back.

Chi Chi Rodriguez, 1970

Through years of experience I have found that air offers less resistance than dirt.

Jack Nicklaus, on why he tees up the ball so high

I'm hitting the woods just great, but I'm having a terrible time getting out of them.

Harry Toscano
Sports Illustrated, 1972

The first yardage stripe is 270 yards. That puts me out before it starts.

Mason Rudolph, at a long-driving contest
Golf Digest, 1974

I know this. If I learn to hit that ball dead straight before I starve, I might rule the world.

Rod Curl, 1975

I only hit the ball about 220 off the tee, but I can always find it.

Bonnie Lauer
Golf Magazine, 1977

It's hard to take a chance when you can't reach the green in the first place.

Tom Kite, on why he doesn't take chances
Sports Illustrated, 1982

I would much rather be hitting the driver and a nine-iron out of the rough than hitting a driver and a four-iron out of the fairway.

Jack Nicklaus
Golf Digest, 1983

If Jack Nicklaus had to play my tee shots, he couldn't break eighty. He'd be a pharmacist with a string of drugstores in Ohio.

Lee Trevino
San Francisco Examiner, 1983

I've built golf courses and laid the irrigation system just by teeing off.

Lee Trevino
"The Tonight Show," NBC-TV, 1983

My goal this year is basically to find the fairways.

Lauri Peterson
San Jose Mercury News, 1983

The woods are full of long hitters.

Harvey Penick, University of Houston golf coach
San Francisco Chronicle, 1984

When I first came out on Tour, I swung all out on every tee shot. My drives finished so far off line, my pants were grass-stained at the knees.

Fuzzy Zoeller
Golf Magazine, 1984

I call my sand wedge my half-Nelson, because I can always strangle the opposition with it.

Byron Nelson
Collier's, 1945

The chip shot from a bunker is like the lapidary's stroke of a diamond.

Henry Cotton, British professional

Actually, the only time I ever took out a one-iron was to kill a tarantula. And I took a seven to do that.

Jim Murray
The Best of Jim Murray, 1965

No Instant Golfer can ever do anything with a two- or three-iron but poke the fire.

Jim Murray

Don't move, hole!

Lee Trevino, hitting an iron at the pin

The good chip is like the good sand trap shot, it's your secret weapon. It allows you to whistle while you walk in the dark alleys of golf.

Tommy Bolt
How to Keep Your Temper on the Golf Course, 1969

I've got the yips—not with my putter, with my wedge.

Lionel Hebert, 1970

You must have a good, fluid swing to make that club pay off. If I catch one of my amateur friends playing with a one-iron he had better be putting with it.

Tommy Bolt
The Hole Truth, 1971

If that's featherin', I'd hate for you to pluck my chickens.

Lee Trevino, to an amateur partner trying to feather an iron shot, 1973

I never leave myself a half shot if I can help it. . . . If I leave myself a tricky little half shot and don't hit it just right over that water, that dog ain't gonna hunt.

Lee Trevino
Golf Digest, 1974

In case you don't know very much about the game of golf, a good one-iron shot is about as easy to come by as an understanding wife.

Dan Jenkins
Dead Solid Perfect, 1974

In golf, you're always thinking about how the course is playing, whether the greens are fast or slow or whether the wind is blowing or dying or shifting. All of a sudden you say, "Aw, just give me a five-iron."

Rex Caldwell
Golf Magazine, 1983

Bibliography

Argea, Angelo, with Jolee Edmondson. *The Bear and I.* New York: Atheneum, 1979.

Armour, Tommy. *A Round of Golf with Tommy Armour.* New York: Simon and Schuster, 1969.

Baker, Stephen. *How to Play Golf in the Low 120's.* Englewood Cliffs, N.J.: Prentice-Hall, 1962.

Ballesteros, Severiano, and Dudley Doust. *Seve: The Young Champion.* New York: Golf Digest, 1984.

Barkow, Al. *Golf's Golden Grind.* New York: Harcourt Brace Jovanovich, 1974.

Bartlett, Michael, ed. *The Golf Book.* New York: Arbor House, 1980.

Beard, Frank. Edited by Dick Schaap. *Pro.* New York: World, 1970.

Beck, Fred. *89 Years in a Sand Trap.* New York: Hill and Wang, 1965.

Bisher, Furman. *The Masters.* Birmingham, Ala.: Oxmoor House, 1976.

———. *The Birth of a Legend.* Englewood Cliffs, N.J.: Prentice-Hall, 1972.

Blalock, Jane, with Dwayne Netland. *The Guts to Win.* Norwalk, Ct.: Golf Digest, 1977.

Bolt, Tommy, with Jimmy Mann. *The Hole Truth.* New York: J. B. Lippincott, 1971.

Bolt, Tommy, with William C. Griffith. *How to Keep Your Temper on the Golf Course.* New York: David McKay, 1969.

Brown, Eric, with Alan Herron. *Out of the Bag.* London, Eng.: Stanley Paul, 1964.

Browning, Robert. *A History of Golf.* London, Eng.: J. M. Dent, 1955.

Campbell, Patrick. *How to Become a Scratch Golfer.* New York: W. W. Norton, 1963.

Chinnock, Frank. *How to Break 90—Consistently!* New York: J. B. Lippincott, 1976.

Davis, William H., ed. *100 Greatest Golf Courses—And Then Some.* New York: Golf Digest, 1982.

Demaret, Jimmy. *My Partner, Ben Hogan.* New York: McGraw-Hill, 1954.

Dobereiner, Peter. *Down the Nineteenth Fairway*. New York: Atheneum, 1983.

——. *The Glorious World of Golf*. New York: McGraw-Hill, 1973.

——. *The World of Golf*. New York: Atheneum, 1981.

Gallwey, W. Timothy. *The Inner Game of Golf*. New York: Random House, 1979.

Gladstone, Dr. Irving A. *Confessions of a Golf Duffer*. New York: Frederick Fell, 1977.

Gleason, Dan. *The Great, The Grand and the Also-Ran*. New York: Random House, 1976.

Graffis, Herb. *The PGA*. New York: Thomas Y. Crowell, 1975.

Gregston, Gene. *Hogan: The Man Who Played for Glory*. Englewood Cliffs, N.J.: Prentice-Hall, 1978.

Gross, Milton. *Eighteen Holes in My Head*. New York: McGraw-Hill, 1959.

Hackett, Buddy. *The Truth About Golf and Other Lies*. Garden City, N.Y.: Doubleday, 1968.

Hagen, Walter, with Margaret Seaton Heck. *The Walter Hagen Story*. New York: Heinemann, 1957.

Herold, Don. *Love That Golf*. New York: A. S. Barnes, 1952.

Hill, Dave, and Nick Seitz. *Teed Off*. Englewood Cliffs, N.J.: Prentice-Hall, 1977.

Hobbs, Michael. *Great Opens*. New York: A. S. Barnes, 1977.

Hobbs, Michael, ed. *In Celebration of Golf*. New York: Charles Scribner's Sons, 1983.

Hope, Bob, with Dwayne Netland. *Confessions of a Hooker*. Garden City, N.Y.: Doubleday, 1985.

Jenkins, Dan. *Dead Solid Perfect*. New York: Atheneum, 1974.

——. *The Dogged Victims of Inexorable Fate*. Boston, Mass.: Little, Brown, 1970.

Johnson, William Oscar, and Nancy P. Williamson. *Whatta-Gal*. Boston, Mass.: Little, Brown, 1975.

Jones, Bob. *British Golf Odyssey*. Monterey, Ca.: Angel Press, 1977.

Jones, Jr., Robert Tyre (Bobby). *Golf Is My Game*. Garden City, N.Y.: Doubleday, 1960.

Keane, Christopher. *The Tour*. New York: Stein and Day, 1974.

Lardner, Rex. *Downhill Lies*. New York: Hawthorn, 1973.

——. *Out of the Bunker and Into the Trees*. New York: Bobbs-Merrill, 1960.

Lema, Tony. *Golfer's Gold*. Boston, Mass.: Little, Brown, 1964.

Longhurst, Henry. Edited by Mark Wilson with Ken Bowden. *The Best of Henry Longhurst*. Norwalk, Conn.: Golf Digest, 1978.

Lopez, Nancy, with Peter Schwed. *The Education of a Woman Golfer*. New York: Simon and Schuster, 1979.

Low, George, with Al Barkow. *The Master of Putting*. New York: Atheneum, 1983.

McCarthy, Colman. *The Pleasures of the Game*. New York: Dial, 1977.

McCormack, Mark H. *Arnie*. New York: Simon and Schuster, 1967.

Miller, Dick. *American's Greatest Golfing Resorts*. New York: Bobbs-Merrill, 1977.

————. *Triumphant Journey*. New York: Holt, Rinehart and Winston, 1980.

Morely, David C. *The Missing Links*. New York: Atheneum, 1976.

Mulvoy, Mark, and Art Spander. *Golf: The Passion and the Challenge*. Englewood Cliffs, N.J.: Prentice-Hall, 1977.

Nicklaus, Jack, with Herbert Warren Wind. *The Greatest Game of All*. New York: Simon and Schuster, 1969.

Palmer, Arnold, with Bob Drum. *Arnold Palmer's Best 54 Golf Holes*. Garden City, N.Y.: Doubleday, 1977.

————, with William Barry Furlong. *Go For Broke*. New York: Simon and Schuster, 1973.

Penna, Toney, with Oscar Fraley. *My Wonderful World of Golf*. New York: Hawthorn, 1965.

Peper, George. *Golf's Supershots*. New York: Atheneum, 1984.

Perry, Paul D. *Billy Casper*. Englewood Cliffs, N.J.: Prentice-Hall, 1969.

Player, Gary, with Floyd Thatcher. *Gary Player*. Waco, Tex.: Word Books, 1974.

Plimpton, George. *The Bogey Man*. New York: Harper & Row, 1968.

Potter, Stephen. *Golfmanship*. New York: McGraw-Hill, 1968.

Price, Charles. *Golfer-At-Large*. New York: Atheneum, 1982.

————. *The World of Golf*. New York: Random House, 1962.

Price, Charles, ed. *The American Golfer*. New York: Random House, 1964.

Puckett, Earl, ed. *Golfer's Digest*. Northfield, Ill.: Digest Books, 1974.

Rees, Dai. *Dai Rees on Golf*. New York: A. S. Barnes, 1959.

Rice, Grantland, with O. B. Keeler. *The Bobby Jones Story*. Atlanta, Ga.: Tupper & Love, 1953.

Roberts, Clifford. *The Story of the Augusta National Golf Club*. Garden City, N.Y.: Doubleday, 1976.

Robertson, James K. *St. Andrews*. Fife, Scot.: Citizen Office, 1967.

Ryde, Peter, ed. *Mostly Golf*. London, Eng.: Adam and Charles Black, 1976.

Sanders, Doug, with Larry Sheehan. *Come Swing with Me*. Garden City, N.Y.: Doubleday, 1974.

Sarazen, Gene, with Herbert Warren Wind. *Thirty Years of Championship Golf.* New York: Prentice-Hall, 1950.

Schaap, Dick. *Massacre at Winged Foot.* New York: Random House, 1974.

————. *The Masters.* New York: Random House, 1970.

Schoor, Gene. *Babe Didrikson.* Garden City, N.Y.: Doubleday, 1978.

Scott, Tom, and Geoffrey Cousins. *The Golf Immortals.* New York: Hart, 1969.

Seitz, Nick, and Bob Toski. *Superstars of Golf.* New York: Golf Digest, 1978.

Sheehan, Larry, ed. *Best Golf Humor from Golf Digest.* New York: Golf Digest, 1972.

————. *Great Golf Humor from Golf Digest.* New York: Golf Digest, 1979.

Snead, Sam, with Al Stump. *The Education of a Golfer.* New York: Simon and Schuster, 1962.

Stanley, Dave, and George G. Ross, eds. *The Golfers Own Book.* New York: Lantern Press, 1956.

Trevino, Lee, and Sam Blair. *They Call Me Super Mex.* New York: Random House, 1982.

Updike, John. *Rabbit Is Rich.* New York: Knopf, 1981.

Venturi, Ken, with Oscar Fraley. *Comeback.* New York: Duell, Sloan and Pearce, 1966.

Wind, Herbert Warren. *Herbert Warren Wind's Golf Book.* New York: Simon and Schuster, 1971.

————. *The Story of American Golf.* New York: Farrar, Straus, 1948.

Wind, Herbert Warren, ed. *The Complete Golfer.* New York: Simon and Schuster, 1954.

Wodehouse, P. G. Edited by D. R. Benson. *Fore!* New York: Ticknor & Fields, 1983.

Index

Diehl, Terry, 137
Dill, Frank, 8
Dillon, George, 167
DiSabella, Karen, 65
Dobereiner, Peter, 36, 48, 60,
    67, 70, 88, 114, 116, 123,
    130, 157, 213, 214, 216, 224
Drum, Bob, 208
Dummett, Robyn, 49
Duncan, George, 73
Dunne, Finley Peter, 23
Dwyer, Mary, 55, 250
Dye, Peter, 36, 37, 72

Eban, Abba, 93
Eichelberger, Dave, 236
Eisenhower, Dwight D., 63, 75,
    143
Elder, Lee, 201
Erfurth, Bill, 189
Evans, Chick, 187

Farrell, Johnny, 153
Faulkner, Max, 17
Ferraris, Jan, 64, 247
Ferraris, Richie, 64
Fields, W. C., 138
Finsterwald, Dow, 18
Fiori, Ed, 213
Fitzgerald, Ray, 89
Fleckman, Marty, 188
Flick, Jim, 122
Floyd, Raymond, 13, 20, 64, 71,
    84, 125, 128, 140, 186, 201
Ford, Doug, 106, 179
Ford, Gerald R., 65, 96
Fought, John, 136
Fox, William Price, 212
Funseth, Rod, 201, 235
Furgol, Ed, 73, 126, 185

Gallico, Paul, 3, 183
Gallwey, W. Timothy, 25, 27,
    185
Gantz, Ivan, 202

Geiberger, Al, 12, 163, 202
George, David Lloyd, 92
Gergen, Joe, 109
Geshwiler, Joe, 39
Gibson, Bob, 90
Gilmore, Tom, 107, 120
Giraudoux, Jean, 35
Gladstone, Irving A., 25
Gleason, Dan, 19, 109, 117, 124,
    178, 190, 199, 201, 216, 218,
    221, 242, 247
Gleason, Jackie, 19, 28, 33, 53
Goldman, David, 178
Goldwater, Barry M., 63
Gordon, Michael, 166
Goulet, Robert, 31
Graffis, Herb, 4, 124, 127, 152,
    231
Graham, Billy, 32, 161
Graham, David, 68, 125
Graham, Lou, 213, 247
Grant, James Edward, 32
Green, Hubert, 109, 136, 202
Grimsley, Will, 206
Gross, Milton, 4, 18, 24, 28, 75,
    81, 98, 239
Grout, Jack, 44
Guzman, Fred, 207

Haas, Jay, 192
Hackett, Buddy, 5, 31, 53, 58,
    82, 144, 198, 242
Hagen, Walter, 9, 23, 44, 62, 86,
    97, 107, 121, 133, 135, 138,
    143, 148, 149, 177, 203, 225,
    238
Hahn, Paul, 30
Halifax, Lord, 171
Hallisey, John, 78
Hamlin, Shelley, 163
Hannigan, Frank, 38, 115, 129
Hardin, Hord, 39, 56
Harlow, Bob, 171, 203
Harmon, Claude, 158, 184

204, 207, 208, 209, 215, 223,
224, 226, 233, 238
Pride, Charley, 32
Pulz, Peanny, 252

Rader, Doug, 90
Raines, Wesley, 167
Rankin, Judy, 230, 247
Ransom, Henry, 97
Ray, Ted, 10
Reagan, Ronald W., 95
Redmond, Jack, 243
Rees, Dai, 57
Reid, Steve, 124
Renner, Jack, 146
Rhoads, Ron, 127
Rice, Grantland, 53, 80, 81, 203,
207
Rice, Jim, 91
Rickles, Don, 32, 195, 196, 213,
218, 220
Riggs, Bobby, 77
Rissel, Carol, 68
Rodgers, Phil, 173, 219
Rodriguez, Chi Chi, 11, 13, 14,
21, 40, 51, 55, 56, 60, 66, 70,
71, 99, 123, 131, 134, 136,
137, 139, 148, 152, 154, 160,
161, 174, 177, 180, 191, 214,
219, 235, 254
Rogers, Will, 80, 86, 93
Roope, George W., 166
Rosburg, Bob, 160, 215
Ross, Mackenzie, 35
Rudolph, Mason, 122, 254
Runyan, Paul, 145, 219
Ruth, Babe, 86

Sanders, Doug, 11, 59, 71, 94,
135, 139, 140, 161, 219, 220,
241
Sanudo, Cesar, 49
Sarazen, Gene, 18, 62, 143, 156,
158, 159, 177, 178, 182, 183,
203, 220, 225, 234

Sayers, Ben, 112
Schaap, Dick, 52, 83, 117, 171,
174, 198, 212
Schenkel, Chris, 117, 196, 210
Schlee, John, 151, 197
Schroeder, John, 221
Schroeder, Ted, 208
Schweizer, Hans, 188
Scully, Vin, 8, 34, 165
Seaver, Tom, 91
Seitz, Nick, 211, 236
Shaw, George Bernard, 69, 176
Shaw, Tom, 235
Sheehan, Larry, 20
Sheehan, Patty, 137, 191, 231,
250
Shepard, Alan, 94
Shepard, Jean, 122
Shor, Toots, 19, 33
Shore, Dinah, 89, 248, 249
Shotten, Burt, 177
Sifford, Charlie, 221
Sikes, Dan, 221, 240
Silvers, Phil, 31
Simmons, Lon, 78, 89
Simpson, Sir Walter, 17, 23, 79,
111, 157, 182, 252
Smith, Alex, 62, 224
Smith, Bubba, 90
Smith, Dave, 188
Smith, Dud, 167
Smith, Horton, 219
Smith, Macdonald, 158, 222
Smith, Red, 42
Snead, J. C., 14, 51, 109, 187,
222
Snead, Sam, 9, 10, 14, 15, 17,
23, 43, 44, 52, 54, 58, 63, 69,
73, 76, 78, 83, 87, 92, 103,
112, 113, 114, 122, 126, 130,
132, 134, 139, 143, 144, 147,
149, 151, 153, 154, 164, 174,
177, 178, 180, 181, 183, 188,
200, 205, 222, 223, 235, 243,
252

Bob Chieger *is a free-lance writer and editor, who has been collecting quotations for nine years. He has worked for several magazines and publishing houses, and his own work has been published in* California, Panorama, Golf, *and the* San Francisco Chronicle. *He is the author of* Voices of Baseball *and* Was It Good for You, Too? *He is single and lives in Seattle, Washington.*

Pat Sullivan *is golf editor and columnist for the* San Francisco Chronicle. *He has been a newsman at* United Press International *and an editor at* Rolling Stone *magazine. His free-lance pieces have been published in* Playboy, The Sporting News, *and* Golf Digest. *Married, with two children, he lives in San Rafael, California.*